MITTEN STRINGS FOR GOD

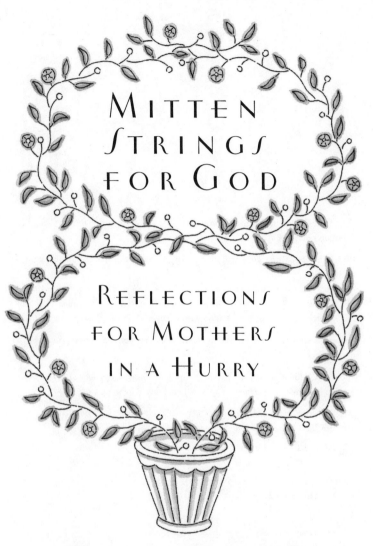

MITTEN STRINGS FOR GOD

REFLECTIONS FOR MOTHERS IN A HURRY

KATRINA KENISON

WARNER BOOKS

A Time Warner Company

Parts of this book have appeared, in somewhat different form, in the following publications:

"Play" as "Mud-pies and Make Believe" in *The Ladies' Home Journal,* June 1999

"Sabbath" as "The Secret of Stressless Sundays" in *Redbook,* September 1999

"Stretching" as "The Secret Ways Kids Change Us" in *Redbook,* November 1999

Grateful acknowledgment is given to Debra Woods for permission to reprint her letter in "Choices."

"For the Children" is by Gary Synder, from *Turtle Island.* Copyright © 1974 by Gary Snyder. Reprinted by permission of New Directions Publishing Corp.

Warner Books, Inc., 1271 Avenue of the Americas, New York, NY 10020
Visit our Web site at www.twbookmark.com

 A Time Warner Company

Printed in the United States of America
First Printing: April 2000
10 9 8 7 6 5 4 3 2 1

Library of Congress Cataloging-in-Publication Data
    Kenison, Katrina.
        Mitten strings for God: reflections for mothers in a hurry / Katrina Kenison.
        p.   cm.
        ISBN 0-446-52531-6
        1. Mothers—Conduct of life.   I. Title.
        BJ1610K462000
        291.4′4′085221—dc21   99-044625

Illustrations by Melanie Marder Parks

FOR HENRY AND JACK, OF COURSE

People travel to wonder at the height of mountains,
at the huge waves of the sea, at the long courses of rivers, at the
vast compass of the ocean, at the circular motion of the stars;
and they pass by themselves without wondering.

—St. Augustine

Contents

MITTEN STRINGS FOR GOD

INTRODUCTION

Each year since our two sons, now nine and six, were born, my husband and I have stayed in touch with family and friends at Christmastime with one of those much maligned "holiday letters." We came to regard it as a necessary stop-gap—the alternative being complete silence—during these hectic years of work and parenthood.

Two Christmases ago, with no major life events to report, I wrote a different kind of letter, describing my own desire to slow life down in the midst of the holiday season and to tune in to a gentler rhythm. I found that in those moments when I did pause long enough to fully experience my own life, my children seemed happier and more peaceful as well. Suddenly, I realized, we truly did have something to celebrate: the joy of real togetherness. These were simple reflections, to be sure, yet, to my surprise, the letter quickly took on a life of its own. Friends and relatives made copies to include in their Christmas cards, and, as a result, people I scarcely knew wrote me letters in return; distant friends, long out of touch, called and wrote, sharing their stories; a writer friend asked if she could reprint the letter in a New Year's Day column; another sent me a subscription to a Quaker newsletter; and an old high school friend (who had received a copy of the letter from his mother, who had received a copy from *mine*) wrote to ask if he might be added to my Christmas card list for the next year. Apparently I had struck a chord.

Being a mother today seems to require that we move too fast most of the time. Much as we may crave quiet interludes with our children, family mealtimes, and meaningful rituals, many of us have resigned ourselves to life without them. There may be days when we barely manage to bring the members of our families together in the same room at the same time—let alone share our innermost thoughts, a joke, or a moment of quiet intimacy.

Yet we also know that our relationships—with ourselves and with each other—need time if they are to flourish. Parents and children alike need time for solitude, time to stretch and think and wonder, time to become acquainted with ourselves and with the world around us. And parents and children need sacred time together, time that is carved out of our busy lives, protected and honored but not scheduled. Time, instead, for just being.

Most of us came of age in a world that was quite different from the one our children now inhabit. As a child I was fed and clothed and loved and cared for—and otherwise left to my own devices a good deal of the time. Even a generation ago, childhood could still be experienced as an accumulation of idle hours, hours in which we were allowed to discover the world for ourselves, piecemeal, and to awaken slowly to its beauty and complexity. In the process, we awakened to ourselves.

We can't reclaim those spacious hours, any more than we can turn back the hands of time and return to that more innocent age. But the lessons taught by the solitude and imposed leisure of childhood are still imprinted on our souls. As children we learned the pleasure of our own company, how to be happy where we were with what we had, how to fill an empty afternoon. But I wonder: Do we give our own children time enough to absorb the subtle teachings of such tranquil moments? Are we granting them the time they need to develop an *inner* life as well as a social one? I remember many, many days when I had nothing *but* time. Yet today I find that I have to struggle to give my own children the very ease and space that I once took for granted.

No, we cannot turn back the hands of time. But as the overworked, exhausted parents of a generation of busy, overstimulated children, we *can* slow down the pace of daily life in our own homes. We can gently reshape lives that have become overstuffed and overly stressful. We can give our children fewer activities and more room in which to breathe, fewer lessons and more time in which to make their own discoveries. We can take a good look at our own maxed-out calendars and crowded lives and let go of the activities and commitments that don't enrich our days. We can be easier on ourselves and demand less of our children. We can protect and honor quiet, unscheduled time, and we can bequeath it to our sons and daughters.

No doubt some of the notions in these pages will seem simple. But I find it is most often the simple gesture or the small goal well met that reaps the greatest reward. And, in our busy lives, it is often the simple gesture that is overlooked, the simple need that is never satisfied. Consider: We figure out a way to chauffeur the kids to their nine lessons a week, to organize the vacation trip to Disney World, and to throw a birthday party for a dozen five-year-olds, complete with costumed mystery guest and party favors. So why does a quiet story told by candlelight seem impossible to manage? In truth, the story—told from the heart and shared in flickering darkness—is more nourishing for our child's soul, and for our own as well, than another soccer practice, an audience with Mickey, or a pile of birthday gifts. We all know this to be true. But sometimes we forget. And sometimes we do need help and inspiration, as we try to negotiate our way from the full-scale chaos of a running-late Monday morning to a place of repose at a child's bedside at the end of the day.

I did not suddenly "see the light" and re-create my life. On the contrary. I began these reflections as I began the Christmas letter that inspired them: out of my own needs as a mother and my desire for more space and harmony in my family. The letter grew into the chapter called "Peace"— and, having begun, I decided to continue, to try to live more deliberately by taking the time to put what I care about into words. I wrote this book because I needed it myself—and because I suspect that I am not alone, that other mothers, too, yearn to offer their children an alternative to our culture's noise, pressures, and materialism.

I've learned that even a small shift in my own thinking usually has a more powerful effect on my day-to-day life than any full-scale attempt at self-improvement. The same is true when it comes to raising children. Holding a vision of their best, true selves in my mind, I suddenly find that the picture has become the reality. We create our lives within our own imaginations well before we ever realize them here on earth. So I imagine what is possible and try to live my days mindfully, and with a sense of humor. This book, then, is not about changing your life. It is about paying more attention to the life you already have, about taking your own life back as you protect your children from the pull of a world that is spinning too fast.

Ultimately, of course, we must each find our own way to be in the world. There are as many ways to live as there are ways to love, and each family has its particular rhythm, its own way of doing and of being. Yet I do believe that, as mothers, we all walk a common path, through a rugged and ineffable territory of love and fury, exhilaration and exhaustion, self-doubt and self-discovery. Every mother I know wishes for close, meaningful relationships with her children, yet none of us is immune to the daily press of obligations and events. We fall captive to the demands of our jobs and families, and to the insistent tug of our fast-paced culture.

And most of us find it increasingly difficult, in the face of all this external pressure, to remember what we already know: True happiness is found within ourselves and in quiet harmony with others. Yet if we let this inner knowledge slip away, our children may never learn it themselves, for we are their first teachers. It is up to each of us to set the example, to show by our own actions our respect for intimacy, contemplation, and wonder. This is perhaps the greatest legacy we can bestow on our children: the capacity to be enchanted by the quiet gifts of everyday life.

Over the years, I have been grateful to all the women who have gone this way before me and have been willing to shine a light upon the trail, that I might find my own way with a bit more confidence. I hope these pages will do the same for other mothers and their children.

Katrina Kenison
July 1999

Dailiness

*W*E HAVE BECOME experts at documenting the lives of our children. From the instant my sons made their first appearances in the delivery room, they have been the stars of our home movies and our favorite photographic subjects. But the most precious moments of my family's life are not the ones illuminated by birthday candles, Christmas lights, or amusement park rides, and they cannot be captured on film or tape.

The moments I hold most dear are those that arise unbidden in the course of any day—small, evanescent, scarcely worth noticing except for the fact that I am being offered, just for a second, a glimpse into another's soul. If my experience as a mother has taught me anything, it is to be awake for such moments, to keep life simple enough to allow them to occur, and to appreciate their fleeting beauty: a lip-smacking good-night "guppy kiss"; a spoonful of maple syrup on snow, served to me in bed with great fanfare on a stormy winter morning; a conversation with a tiny speckled salamander discovered, blinking calmly, under a rock. . . . These are the moments that, woven together, constitute the unique fabric of our family life. Herein lies the deep color, the lights and shadows, of our days together.

I am fortunate to have had a mentor in the art of living in the moment. In fact, I received my most precious lesson from her after her death. My older son, Henry, was a year and a half old, and I had left him for the first time, to spend four days in Atlanta, going through the papers of my friend Olive Ann Burns. When Olive Ann and I had first met, eight years earlier, I was an ambitious twenty-five-year-old, eager to make my way in the world of New York publishing. She was a sixty-year-old housewife about to publish her first novel after a ten-year battle with cancer. In retrospect, I suppose I was of some small help to Olive Ann, suggesting ways to cut pages from her enormous manuscript or sharpen a character, but I now know that she had much more to offer me, namely an unforgettable example of how life ought to be lived, even in the face of tremendous pain.

Cold Sassy Tree surprised everyone by becoming a best-seller, and Olive Ann Burns became a national celebrity. Having been confined to the house during all those years of illness, she thoroughly enjoyed her moment in the spotlight. But it was not to last. Soon after she embarked on a sequel to *Cold Sassy Tree,* her cancer returned. Although she continued to write, and later to dictate, from her bed, the book was unfinished when she died on July 4, 1990.

By the time of Olive Ann's death, I had left publishing to edit an annual short-story anthology from home. Much as I had loved my career, I knew that I could not sustain that kind of commitment to my work and to children, too. But my relationship with Olive Ann had long since transcended that between editor and writer. She was my friend and my teacher as well, for she embodied the kind of courage and spirit that I aspired to. On the other side, she had come to trust my editorial judgment, and she knew that I would be honest with her about the new book.

Olive Ann had completed twelve chapters when she died and had made notes for others. She had also left explicit wishes for the manuscript: She wanted it to be published somehow, so that the hundreds of people who had written her asking for a sequel would not feel let down. Olive Ann had told me this story many times; we had sat side by side on her couch as she showed me the family photo album, introducing me to the real-life characters who had inspired her work. So, with her family's encouragement, I agreed to supplement Olive Ann's chapters with a reminiscence of their author, telling how *Cold Sassy Tree* came to be written and fleshing out the story of the sequel. This was the task that brought me to Atlanta.

Every mother remembers the first night she spends away from her first child. Settling into the familiar little inn a few blocks from Olive Ann's house, where I had always stayed when visiting her, I felt that I had been yanked out of my current life, as a wife and mother, and hurled back into my former one. I was rereading *Cold Sassy Tree* as preparation for the work ahead, and—wonder of wonders—I was alone. For the first time since my son was born, I had time to reflect, to become reacquainted with myself, apart from my husband and my baby. I tried to appreciate the solitude, for I had always loved it, but now I felt unmoored, free-floating in a hotel room while my real life went on without me, someplace else. I realized how grateful I was for all the connections that usually held me in place, and I couldn't wait to get home.

It was in this mood that I sat down in the middle of a room filled with Olive Ann. There were all the drafts of *Cold Sassy Tree*, every typed page densely scribbled with her revisions; there were boxes of fan mail; manuscript pages of the new book, ideas she had jotted on the backs of envelopes and shopping lists, love letters from her late husband, and, perhaps most poignant of all, notes Olive Ann had written to herself to bolster her own courage during the hard times.

Late in the afternoon of my last day in Atlanta, I came across a sheet of yellow-lined paper on which Olive Ann had written these words:

I have learned to quit speeding through life, always trying to do too many things too quickly, without taking the time to enjoy each day's doings. I think I always thought of real living as being high. I don't mean on drugs—I mean real living was falling in love, or when I got my first job, or when I was able to help somebody, or watch my baby get born, or have a good morning of really good writing. In between the highs I was impatient—you know how it is—life seemed so Daily. Now I love the dailiness. I enjoy washing dishes. I enjoy cooking, I see my father's roses out the kitchen window, I like picking beans. I notice everything—birdsongs, the clouds, the sound of wind, the glory of sunshine after two weeks of rain. These things I took for granted before.

It seemed that Olive Ann was speaking directly to me. I copied the lines down and then taped them above my desk when I got home, where they remain to this day. For many weeks I found myself blinking back tears every time I read them, for my own life with an infant was about nothing if not "dailiness," but mine was just beginning, while hers had ended. The fact that she was gone was a powerful reminder to me to pay attention while I had the chance, and to respect the fact that our time here is short.

In a way, those words launched me on the journey into what I have come to feel is my authentic adult life. The idea of living in the moment is not new, of course, but the piece of paper that I carried home from Atlanta and hung above my desk was the inspiration I needed to begin to turn an idea into a way of life. Those simple words seemed to hold out to me a practice, a way of being, that was worth striving for. I didn't want to learn this lesson as a result of ten years of cancer and a few brushes with mortality, as Olive Ann had done—I wanted to learn it now, to be aware of life's beauty even before fate threatened to take it away.

Ours is a society that places high value on achievement and acquisition. The subtle rewards of contemplation, quiet, and deep connection with another human being are held in low esteem, if they are recognized at all. As a result, mothers are constantly pulled in two directions: Can we negotiate the demands of our careers and the world at large, and meet our own emotional and physical needs—not to mention those of our children—at the same time? Can we keep our sights on what is important in any given moment? Do we know how to shut the door, stop the noise, and tune in to our own inner lives?

We all have fallen victim at one time or another to the relentless cycle of our children's playdates and after-school lessons, to the push for their academic and athletic accomplishments, and to their endless desires for the latest toy, video game, or designer sneakers. The adage of our age seems to be "Get more out of life!" And we do our best to obey. Grab a snack, round up the kids, and we're out the door—to do, or buy, or learn something more.

But in our efforts to make each moment "count," we seem to have lost the knack of appreciating the ordinary. We provide our children with so much that the extraordinary isn't special anymore, and the subtle rhythms of daily life elude us altogether. We do too much and savor too little. We mistake activity for happiness, and so we stuff our children's days with activities, and their heads with information, when we ought to be feeding their souls instead. I know a mother who came upon her two-year-old sitting alone, lost in a daydream, and worried that he was "wasting time."

Over the years, I *have* learned to quit speeding through life, but it is a lesson I must take up and learn again every day, for the world conspires to keep us all moving fast. I have found that it is much easier for me to stay busy than to make a commitment to empty time—not surprising, perhaps, in a culture that seems to equate being busy with being alive. Yet if we don't attend to life's small rituals, if we can't find time to savor "dailiness," then we really are impoverished. Our agendas starve our souls.

Like all mothers, I harbor dreams for my children, and sometimes I fall under the spell of my own aspirations for them. We want our children to do well! But when I stop and think about what I *truly* want for them, I know that it is not material wealth or academic brilliance or athletic prowess. My deeper hope is that each of my sons will be able to see the sacred in the ordinary; that they, too, will grow up knowing how to "love the dailiness." So, for their sakes as well as my own, I remind myself to slow down and enjoy the day's doings. The daily rhythms of life, the humble household rituals, the nourishment I provide—these are my offerings to my children, given with love and gratefully received.

When I stop speeding through life, I find the joy in each day's doings, in the life that cannot be bought, but only discovered, created, savored, and lived.

MORNING

USUALLY HENRY IS first, slipping silently into our bed before first light, sometimes even falling back to sleep nestled into the curve of his father's back. Before long, Jack pads in. Hugging his pillow, still half-asleep, he trusts that he will find his way right into my arms, be lifted up, settled, and wrapped in hugs and goose down. Soon the furnace shudders to life. By the time I touch toes to floor, the room will be warm; the house is getting ready for us. Outside the window at the foot of the bed, the first pale washes of color seep across the sky. Here is a moment of stillness, still wrapped in dreams, before the day ahead begins to take shape in my mind—appointments to keep, plans for my work, the children's schedules, and, too, my own aspirations for this day.

In the end, it is not children but crows who really bring me to my senses. They jeer and clamor over their dawn breakfasts like a bunch of rowdy construction workers jazzed up on too much coffee. And then the first words of the morning are spoken. Who can ever remember, later, what they were? (Today, Jack: "Well, now it's only nineteen more days until my birthday!") Whether they are memorable or mundane, spontaneous or considered, the words that break night's silent spell are nevertheless the beginning of something new, another day in the life of our family. Perhaps it is a beginning we take for granted, or don't even recognize as such. Some mornings we all leap from the bed, already late, our thoughts rushing ahead to the world beyond our own front door.

But I cheat myself if I fail to give the morning its due. For these first waking minutes can affect the quality of the entire day, determining the way things will go for each one of us. It is a tender time. Our souls, returning from their mysterious sojourns of the night, must now become grounded once again in the here and now and the concerns of the day. If I am conscious enough to honor this process—greeting my husband and children with hugs and kisses and gentle words—then each one of us may actually experience the sense of renewal that each day offers. The mistakes of yesterday are forgiven, regrets put aside. Here, in the day's first hushed moments, our family can come together again in loving spirit, rested and refreshed.

Before my husband and I had children, the early morning was a time for the two of us to wrap our arms around each other and talk with an intimacy and honesty that didn't seem possible at any other time. During those first vulnerable moments after waking, we could share our fears, open our hearts, laugh, and dream together. With the arrival of our first baby, though, mornings suddenly began in darkness, before either of us was quite ready, so we began bringing our early riser into bed with us, in hopes of finding a few more minutes of sleep. Now, nearly ten years later, there are four of us in bed each morning, a tangle of arms and legs, hands and feet, warm bodies and waking hearts.

Someday our boys will decide that they have grown too old to climb into bed with Mom and Dad for cuddles before the work of the day begins. Till then, though, I will cherish this morning ritual, our small universe of four, the sweet comfort of embrace.

Last fall, at a friend's lakeside cabin, we rolled out of sleeping bags and crept outside, one by one, at sunrise. In fact, the outhouse was our dawn destination. But the sight of the morning mist, rising off the water in golden tendrils, caught each of us. There, for a silent, grateful moment, I stood with my husband and my children, shivering with cold, and greeted the day. At home, of course, nature calls and we need venture only as far as the indoor plumbing requires. Yet we can still pause long enough to gaze at the new world before our eyes and to give thanks for the day we have been given. Then, in a blink, we are scattered—by a fit of the giggles or the day's first sibling battle; by the clatter of breakfast dishes and the general commotion that ensues as everyone gets up and out the door. But at least, as we set forth, we each carry within us the day's first gift, a quiet, holy moment born of love.

Greeting the day, we welcome each
other back into the world.

PEACE

*I*T IS SUNDAY afternoon. Jack is curled up in the crook of my arm, having decided to finger-knit a whole ball of yarn while I crochet mitten strings for all of our surviving pairs. We have been quiet, absorbed in our work, for quite some time when he asks, "This is peace, isn't it?" I agree that it is indeed. "I love this peace," he says.

So often we bemoan our children's hyperactivity and short fuses. But what kind of example do we set for them as we race from here to there ourselves, trying to accomplish more, have more, experience more, in the course of a day? My rambunctious five-year-old actually craves stillness, embraces it gratefully, whenever I stop long enough to create it with him.

As the mother of two lively boys, I am forever seeking a balance in our family life between activity and stillness, sound and silence, society and solitude. For now, I still have a measure of control over the tenor of my children's days, but as the actual amount of time we spend alone together inevitably shrinks, maintaining this balance becomes even more important—and more challenging. Certainly there can be a very wide gap between my vision of harmonious family life and the day-to-day reality. Many days we simply throw a handful of balls up in the air and start juggling: work, school, music lessons, swimming lessons, volunteer work, playdates for the kids and social obligations for Mom and Dad, school meetings, housework, homework . . . The list goes on.

Most of the mothers I know are performing some variation on this theme. That we are also efficiency experts almost goes without saying. How else could we meet our deadlines, care for our children, make time for our partners, and put dinner on the table every night?

Yet most of us also yearn for a quality in our lives that has nothing to do with these accomplishments. It might be a desire for grace or spaciousness, for a sense of deeper connection with the universe, or simply, as Jack said, for peace. It is a quality that we know to be essential in our children's lives—and yet is all too often missing from our own.

We *do* live on the run so much of the time, in too great a hurry to shape and enjoy the kinds of meaningful interactions that define a family's life and nurture each of its members. Only by slowing down do we make time for one another. Only by stopping long enough to observe our surroundings can we bring form and meaning to our lives and make the small adjustments needed to stay on course.

Our children need this kind of pause, too. Regular rest for the spirit is as necessary for their healthy growth as sleep, fresh air, and good food. And just as our children depend on us for three meals a day, they also need us to prepare peaceful spaces for them in the midst of this busy world.

When we create a haven of serenity—be it in a quiet room, by means of a simple ritual, or even in the space of a fleeting moment—we make room for spirit. I do not want my children to experience their lives as a dash from one thing to the next. I do not want them to be bombarded with noise, information, and media messages, to be pulled along on a current of activity and stimulation. They need time to stop and exhale, time to feel centered, safe, and whole.

For me, the winter holidays are always a time of mounting tension—both children's birthdays in quick succession, Thanksgiving and Christmas to orchestrate, and my annual work deadline at the end of January, which is always a mad race to the finish. This year, having taken on more work than usual, I felt the crunch even earlier—and my tension seemed to be as contagious as a winter cold. When I am feeling rushed, overworked, and stressed, that quality seeps into the very air around me; everyone else is on edge, too.

At the same time, Jack is confronting his own challenges as he struggles to negotiate the first months of kindergarten. His life has become more complicated, with longer school days, more expectations to meet, and a widening gap between him and his older brother, who suddenly prefers reading books behind closed doors to games of "let's pretend." An overextended mother and a wound-up five-year-old can be an incendiary combination, and I'm afraid we have both suffered.

Now, as the holiday rush begins to gather speed, I am worrying about deadlines, fighting a sore throat, and overwhelmed by the prospect of Christmas. On top of everything else, I simply cannot bear to think about gifts to buy and wrap. Instead, these days, I find myself thinking about gifts of time; of our family's need to be quiet together in the midst of all the seasonal events and expectations. Yes, I could continue to struggle against the cold weather and short days as I race from one holiday chore to the next. Or I could take my cue from nature and accept the earth's invitation to slow down. I could choose to do less out in the world and to spend more time sequestered inside, nestled in with my children, hot cocoa and books, mail-order catalogs and afghans.

*L*ike Thoreau, I love "a broad margin to my life"—the less packed into a day, the better. Sitting still, I am able to appreciate my life simply because I am taking the time to experience it. But even a few moments of tranquillity can be hard won. It seems that idleness is suspect; we are supposed to be on the go. Perhaps that is why I am always so grateful for the small clearings that can suddenly appear even in the midst of a busy day. These accidental, hallowed scraps of time offer us a break from the outside world, at least for a few moments. Arriving ten minutes early for a piano lesson, the boys flop down outside on a patch of fresh powder, waving arms and legs to etch a row of ragged angels into the snow. Informed that our pediatrician is running an hour behind schedule, we dash back out to the car, crawl into the back, and tell a story while rain pounds on the roof. Or someone suggests tea before bed, and we all gather round the table, light a candle, and drink in the night.

Having reaped the blessings of these accidental moments of grace, I am learning to leave some space around the edges of our days. There is no peace to be found in our culture. So I try to build the margins in, to keep our days from being inscribed too densely. Some days seem to offer their own quality of space and ease. Other times I have to switch gears midway through—postponing the errands, canceling a playdate, ordering pizza for dinner, skipping an evening meeting—so that I can pull my children out of the swift current of a day and guide them into a calm pool instead.

In a society that endorses activity, I think we would all do well to put more trust in stillness. No matter how busy we are, we can find meaning and renewal in those moments that are available to us. We can come together in an intimate way, even at the end of a long, draining day, if we are willing to be fully present with our children—to take the time to hear their confidences and to respond from the heart. We can teach them the value of a deep breath, of a spiritual pause, of rest, if we take the time to learn it ourselves.

When I come to a stop myself, when I draw a circle of stillness around me, my children are drawn into that peaceful place. They visibly relax, as if my very calmness nourishes them. The impact of just a few minutes of quiet attention can be profound, changing the mood of an entire day, restoring equilibrium to a distressed child, and to a frazzled mother as well.

We might sit side by side and draw, or gather up a stack of favorite old picture books and read them, make strange creatures out of clay, or just cuddle on the couch and listen to music as darkness falls. These are the moments when my children reveal themselves to me, when conversation spirals up and out, from the here and now into the realm of spirit and imagination. There, in that place Tennyson calls the "quiet limit of the world," we connect with one another at a very deep soul level. My children know then that they have my full attention and, even more important, that there's no other place I'd rather be at that moment.

*A*s I finish my mitten strings and put them into the sewing basket, we look up and see snow-flakes drifting past the window. Jack holds out his very long piece of blue yarn. "I'm knitting a mitten string for God," he says. Peace.

In stillness, we find our peace. Knowing peace
at home, we bring peace into the world.

QUIET

THERE IS MUZAK on the other end of the telephone hold line, the fax line is ringing, and my computer is beeping to tell me I have mail. TVs are everywhere. Our health clubs, doctors' offices, restaurants, stores, supermarkets, and airports are wired for sound. If I venture too close to that BMW in the parking garage, an electronic voice warns me to keep my distance. The self-service gas pumps talk back. Tickle Elmo, and he will laugh—loudly. Furby speaks up in the middle of the night. Children's catalogs promote lullaby tapes, stories on tape, and even meditation tapes for toddlers. As I write these words, the neighbor's lawn crew is launching into a full-scale attack next door, assaulting the yard—and my senses—

with their high-powered leaf blowers, weed whackers, and industrial mowers. . . .

How did our world get so noisy? Have we grown so accustomed to the incessant background noise of our daily lives that we have forgotten the shape and feel and sound of silence? Even under their own roofs, many families today are separated from one another by the thrum of computers, the canned noise of competing TVs, ringing phones, and omnipresent background music from radios and CD players.

Yet most of us do appreciate silence. Think of the quiet that falls over the house in the moments just after the children are asleep; of a sunset at the beach, with only your own thoughts for company; of the richly textured stillness of an empty church or synagogue. Unfortunately, though, we seem to have forgotten silence's value. Our days are so filled with activity, noise, and commotion that we have come to equate sound with life. Little by little we have brought our stereo speakers, telephones, and TVs into every room of the house. And how easily the decibel levels rise! When adults and children have to compete with a sound track just to be heard, everyone ends up shouting—and the noise level goes up even higher. One friend admitted, "I don't think my kids even know *how* to talk in a normal tone of voice!" But there is intimacy in a whisper, pools of meaning in the empty spaces between our words, sustenance in quiet.

Certainly the noise level of modern life is undesirable for adults, for when every waking moment is colored by sound, we lose touch with our bodies and our own inner selves. We literally can't hear ourselves think. But a noisy environment is even more insidious for children. Children are easily pulled out of themselves by whatever is going on around them. Today, many of our children have no firsthand experience of silence. They are as overstimulated as their stressed-out parents. Little wonder, then, that attention disorders are on the rise or that our children seem so easily distracted. Raised on a steady diet of noise and media stimulation, many children simply don't know what it feels like to be at rest in their own quiet centers.

*I*f we are to feed others, we must first be fed ourselves. We must embrace quiet ourselves before we can bring it to our children. I know that I need quiet time each day to draw myself together. And I have come to realize that my children need this kind of time as well, time when they can be fully present with themselves. Time to discern and follow their own rhythm, time in which to create their own music. In fact, I have a friend who rarely plays any recorded music in her home, for this very reason. "If my daughter is listening to tapes or CDs," she explains, "that means she's just taking something in, instead of generating something of her own. I would rather hear her singing her own songs."

I am convinced that the simplest, most effective way to enrich family life is to return quiet to our homes. When my husband and I set up housekeeping together, his clock radio came on each morning at six-thirty, tuned to a local all-news station. For the first week I awakened to the lurid, live details of that day's first automobile crash. Finally I spoke up. He was surprised that these images actually bothered me; I was shocked that he would choose to wake up to them. We compromised then by switching to a classical music station. Now, over a dozen years later, we don't even keep a clock in the bedroom, let alone a radio. Once called upon, our inner clocks became reliable timekeepers. It's not that I won the battle, but simply that as we both became more and more conscious of the words, sounds, and images we were willing to allow into our lives, we eliminated virtually everything that we don't consider valuable.

This is not to say we live in complete silence—far from it. Our home is filled with music and laughter and, yes, noise. But it is noise of our own making, or noise of our own choosing—and we are very choosy! In each day there are long stretches of quiet. I often cook, garden, write, and read in silence. Our boys draw, paint, do puzzles and projects—in silence. Before we flick on the car radio or the CD player, we stop long enough to think: Do we want to exchange this quiet for sound? Sometimes the answer is yes, but not always. Last week I sang along to my favorite Grateful Dead CD as I prepared a birthday feast for my husband;

today, by everyone's unspoken agreement, the quiet in this house was broken only by the sounds of our own voices. I agree with Madeleine L'Engle, who says, "We need both for our full development: the joy of the sense of sound; and the equally great joy of its absence."

*B*eing quiet in an age of noise—machine noise, advertising noise, electronic noise, even noise masquerading as music—is an affirmation of a belief in something deeper and more precious: the real world and the miracle of our existence in it, moment to moment. In silence, I become attentive. I see more: the slant of light across the kitchen table, the jewel-toned nasturtiums in their vase on the sill, the tentative expression on one son's early-morning face, the ready-for-anything entrance of the other. I hear more, too: the breeze outside the window, eggs sizzling in the pan, a child singing in an upstairs bedroom, another's slow step on the back stair. In fact, I am fully attuned to all of these sounds, for they constitute the melody of this day, the music that tells me who we are and what we need, where we've been and where we're headed.

If the noise of modern life has seeped into every corner of your home, try clearing a space for silence.

- ∾ Be conscious of all the different kinds of noise you allow into your life. Begin to eliminate any that don't enhance the present moment.

- ∾ Start and end each day with a time of quiet throughout your home.

- ∾ Protect your children from noise overdoses. Allow them to grow in—and to grow into—silence.

- ∾ Avoid electronic games and toys that talk, beep, or make other noises. The best sound effects are those that children make themselves.

- ∾ Begin meals with "quiet bites," a few minutes of centering silence. Then enjoy one another's company without the accompaniment of TV or CD player.

- ∾ Turn off the sound track in your life. If your family has grown accustomed to television or music as background noise, experiment with intervals of silence.

*I*n his book *Care of the Soul,* Thomas Moore observes that "a common symptom of modern life is that there is no time for thought, or even for letting the impressions of a day sink in. Yet it is only when the world enters the heart that it can be made into soul. The vessel in which soulmaking takes place is an inner container, scooped out by reflection and wonder."

This morning Jack came to me with a song. "I thought of it while I was looking out my bedroom window," he explained. And then, very sweetly, he sang,

> *I am as high as an airplane*
> *I am a cloud so high*
> *As high as an airplane can go*
> *Oh, I love you now*

In silence, we allow the world to enter our hearts. We can learn to be quiet with the people we most love, reweaving our connections without words. And we can tune in to the sounds we wish to live by, the sounds that will, after all, determine our very sense of well-being. For me, they include the infinite variety of birdsong at first light; the snap of logs in the woodstove; the rippling music of wind chimes on the back porch; our son playing piano each morning after breakfast; a neighbor's old-fashioned dinner gong, reverberating through our backyard every night at six. . . . These are the sound markers of my days, as beautiful and as precious to me as a symphony by Beethoven.

When we cultivate a mood of calm repose in our homes, we are scooping out a space for reflection and wonder, for contemplation and reverie. Our children are exposed to incessant commotion in the world that exists beyond our walls. Let home be the place where they can find the peace and quiet they need to make sense of it all. A place, too, where we can nurture our inner lives without distraction. The soul speaks softly. And so I guard our quiet times. Creativity flourishes in these spaces; grace and peace reside here, too.

When I clear a quiet space for my family,
I make room for our souls to grow.

ʃIMPLICITY

*T*WO WEEKS BEFORE Easter, I visit a friend whose children are the same age as mine. When I arrive, she is just cleaning up after an afternoon of coloring eggs with her son and daughter. There are Ukrainian masterpieces, painstakingly created with special tools, dyes, and wax. In addition, they have made stenciled eggs, brilliant glitter eggs, and marbelized eggs, all from kits ordered from a catalog. Some of the eggs feature paintings of flowers and bunnies. Others have been blown out, colored with vegetable dye, and arranged in a basket filled with real, growing grass, planted in March so that it would reach its peak for Easter weekend.

While the children head outside to play, my friend sweeps glitter off the floor, scrubs the table, and washes tiny paintbrushes. The results of their labors are breathtaking, and I ooh and ahh over every egg. They *are* beautiful. But, she confesses with a sigh, she has done most of them herself. The Ukrainian kit proved too complicated for the kids, and the stencils were difficult to do. The children each made a couple of glitter eggs, but they ended up with glue all over their hands and soon lost interest. "Next year," my friend says, laughing, "we're going back to the basic $2.99 kit from CVS!"

I think of those Easter eggs now as I set out to write about simplicity. So often, it seems, *we* are the ones who make our own lives more complicated than they need to be. We set the bar too high, take on too much, turn small doings into big ones. In part the culture is to blame—as each holiday rolls around, we confront an ever-expanding array of merchandise to go with it. There is more to see, more to do, more to buy, than ever before. And how easy it is to fall into thinking that living well means partaking of all that's offered. With so many options and opportunities to choose from, it can be a challenge just figuring out where to draw the line.

Why settle for food coloring and vinegar when you can create an artistic treasure instead? Why stop at birthday cake and ice cream at home when you can rent an indoor playground and invite the whole class? Why spend the Saturday before Christmas sledding with the family when you could all be attending the annual downtown holiday extravaganza?

Why indeed? The fact is, the marketers of this world have gotten very good at thinking of new ways to create desires for goods and services and experiences that didn't even exist a generation ago. As a result, we end up offering too much to our children and taking on too much ourselves.

It is not enough, anymore, to pull together a Halloween costume from the dress-up bin, add a few extra touches, and head out the door to go trick-or-treating. The store-bought costumes are more elaborate, more expensive, and more grisly every year. There are decorations to buy, light shows to orchestrate on the front lawn, haunted houses to visit, and a week's worth of pre-Halloween activities to attend. Last fall my neighbor's six-year-old daughter had been in and out of her costume so many times that she refused to put it back on for Halloween night. She'd been a ballerina in a parade, at school, and at two parties. The novelty had worn off.

I know a little boy who pitched a tantrum at the end of an elaborate birthday party because his goody bag didn't have enough treats in it. At another, children scrambled on all fours to pick up candy scattered from a piñata and then protested because there wasn't enough. Over the past couple of years, my boys have attended birthdays featuring pony rides, a visit from Batman, wild animals, indoor rock climbing, gymnastics, and an inflated space jump, rented by the hour. I've seen overexcited kids fall apart and more than one exhausted mother weeping in the kitchen.

*W*hat message do our own excesses send to our children? In our efforts to create special occasions for them, are we losing sight of what's really important? Are these elaborate productions crowding out the kinds of simple, heartfelt celebrations that truly enrich our lives and delight our children?

A few weeks ago, a well-known storyteller came to our town. I made the plans: Jack and a friend would have an early dinner at our house, and then we would enjoy an evening of stories downtown. We ate at five-thirty, bundled into boots and raincoats, and set out in a downpour. The library meeting room was full of wet, boisterous children, ranging in age from two to thirteen—a tough audience at the best of times. But this was six-thirty, mothers were worn out and bedraggled, and the children were rollicking with energy. I hoped that our storytelling celebrity would dim the fluorescent lights, gather the children into a circle, bring a hush to the crowded room. But, it seemed, the mood was already set, and that was what he played to, unleashing a torrent of voices, antics, and impersonations in an effort to capture the attention of this scattered group.

"How come no one is listening?" whispered Jack.

"I think it's past my bedtime," confided four-year-old Nick.

And I had to ask myself, What on earth are we doing here?

Of course, hindsight is easy. But had I brought a little more thought to our agenda that evening, I would have realized that these two small children did not require an outing in order to experience something special. How much better off we would have been staying home on that stormy night, lighting a fire in the fireplace, and inviting Jack's friend for dinner and a story told by firelight in our own living room. Once again I was reminded: If I pause long enough to listen to my own inner voice, rather than heeding some external call to go, see, and do, I make better choices for us all.

It takes conviction to say, "This is enough"—whether it be enough holiday events, enough guests at a party, enough presents, or simply enough activities for next Saturday. And it is hard to feel confidence in our own choices, in our own sense of limits, when everyone around us seems convinced that more and bigger is better.

But I am learning. When I find myself worrying, Can I pull this whole thing off? instead of looking forward to a special day, I know it's because I have allowed an event to become more extravagant and ambitious than it needs to be. There is another way. We don't have to make everything into such a big deal. We can choose simplicity over complication. And what relief there is in simplicity. Here's a start:

⁓ Downscale holiday celebrations. Keep the focus on family, on meaningful rituals and traditions, and on simple activities. Give fewer gifts, and take more time to enjoy them. One year we bought Christmas presents for a needy family and agreed that we would pay for those gifts by scaling down our own giving to one gift per person. No one felt deprived; in fact, I think we all felt relieved. When I ask my children what they love most about our Christmas, their answers remind me that simple really is best: reading our Christmas books, the advent calendar, our annual carol sing with the family next door, lighting the ting-a-ling on Christmas Eve. . . .

~ Set a limit on holiday activities. (One Easter egg hunt is enough!)

~ Don't feel guilty about skipping events that everyone else attends. Your children need you and your attention, not more activities. Last year we didn't go to the end-of-the-year barbecue and pool party for Henry's second-grade class—simply because we needed a quiet family day more than we needed one more end-of-school event. As I remind my children when the birthday party invitations start to pile up, "You don't have to go to everything." Watching us manage our own lives sensibly, our children will learn to set limits, too.

~ Celebrate birthdays in a way that honors the qualities you love in your child. They don't have to be big productions; make them expressions of love instead: a special meal, an outing with a friend, a birthday ritual carried on year after year. My sons each have a birthday candle waiting for them on the breakfast table; at dinnertime, each family member offers a birthday wish for the coming year.

~ Whether you're decorating the Christmas tree, making latkes, or coloring Easter eggs, remember that the process is more important for your child than the outcome. Keep the process simple, and your child will enjoy it more.

~ Set limits and stick to them. In our house, no one is allowed to wear their Halloween costumes until Halloween night. Although it's hard for the kids to wait, it's worth it. The anticipation builds, and Halloween lasts for a few hours instead of a whole week. Does anyone really want a week of Halloween?

~ You don't have to prove anything to anybody. Christmas is not a competition, a seder is not a cooking contest, a birthday doesn't need to be a blowout, a dinner party can be potluck.

~ Celebrate small blessings and offbeat occasions. Once we take the pressure off ourselves to do things in a big way, we find more reasons to celebrate life's little moments. Jack and I once made a birthday cake for Curious George. Half birthdays are reason enough to enjoy a special meal. Hot summer days suggest impromptu lemonade parties. For children, every day holds potential for celebration and ceremony—the first day of spring, the first snowfall, the harvest moon. A song, a poem read aloud, a ritual, or a special snack—it doesn't take much to create a celebration that affirms life and connects us to the natural order of things: animals, wind, sky, and earth.

*Y*esterday we colored our own Easter eggs. Taking my friend's experience to heart, I kept it simple. Five bowls of colored water. There was magic enough in that.

> *In simplicity there is freedom—*
> *freedom to do less and to enjoy more.*

TV

I WAS LOOKING AFTER a little boy in our neighborhood until his mom got home from work. Jake and Henry played catch outside for a while, then came in and drew. After an hour or so Henry came downstairs. "Mom," he said, "Jake wants to watch a movie, and when I told him that we couldn't, and that we don't even watch TV, you know what he said? He said, 'No TV? How do you *live*?' "

"What did you say?" I asked.

"Well," said Henry, "I told him we just live."

*I*t has been four years since my husband and I agreed that, instead of arguing with our kids about how much TV they were allowed to watch, we would simply turn the TV off altogether. Since that time we have rented an occasional video, and the boys have watched the odd TV show at Grandma's house or in the homes of relatives and friends. But by and large, TV is simply not a part of our lives. It has been a nonissue for so long that none of us even think about it anymore. Perhaps that's why I've found it hard to know where to begin this piece about television and the media. My feelings on the subject have, if anything, grown stronger, but our TV set has been gathering dust for quite a while now. It has lost its power over all of us.

So tonight I set out for a walk, to gather my thoughts. Jack followed me outside, and we lay pressed against one another in the lawn chair for a half hour before his bedtime, watching the bats fly out against a darkening sky. They give us the shivers, these nocturnal neighbors of ours, and it is a delicious thrill to be out there with them, whispering like trespassers in our own backyard while they lay claim to the night. Finally it was too dark to see the bats darting above our heads any longer. The sky was strewn with stars by then, and we made wishes. "I wish I could see everything in the whole world," said Jack, "Mt. Everest, and Madagascar, and Australia, and China."

"Maybe you will see those places someday," I said.

"It's amazing to think," he went on, "that all those places really exist, and that people are living there right now, under this very same sky and under this very same moon."

We lay there in the chair for a little while more, pondering the vastness of life, until goose bumps crept up our arms. I took Jack inside to bed and headed out again. As I walked through the neighborhood, still treasuring those sweet moments with my son, I began to count the bluish lights flickering in every living room I passed. Was there any house where the television wasn't on? A house in which a family was simply enjoying one another's company or drinking in the sounds and smells of this spring evening? I didn't see one.

Our lives are a series of choices. Some we deliberate over, others we make automatically. But as we begin to live our lives more consciously, with more attention to the details, we become increasingly aware of just how many decisions we do make in the course of every day—from what we toss into our grocery carts to the images we allow into our living rooms. We begin to choose foods that promote healthy bodies and, in the same way, we begin to choose sensory experiences that nurture our souls. Knowing that the shape and mood we bring to a day has a deep effect on our children's own sense of well-being, we begin to pay more attention to the atmosphere in our homes. We may become more thoughtful in our words and gestures, more deliberate as we attend to our surroundings. The challenge, of course, is to make our choices creatively, so that the details of our lives support and nourish what is best in us.

As I rounded the block and headed toward home to-night, I could not help but feel a bit sad, discouraged to think how easily we have come to accept the pervasiveness of the media in our lives. The world we live in is a world of our own making, the sum of all our collective choices. Yet so many parents feel powerless to make good choices, sensing that the pull of the media is stronger than they are. How can any of us protect our children from the relentless display of violence, sex, noise, inappropriate humor, and advertising in a media-driven world that is already saturated with these sounds and images? How will our children resist such influences if we can't manage to resist them ourselves? How is it that, in a society in which most of us feel starved for time, we are willing to hand over the time we *do* have to our TV sets? On this velvety night of bats and stars and apple blossoms, TV had taken its captives.

Several years ago, columnist Ellen Goodman suggested that thoughtful parents have become the real counterculture in our society; that is, they counter the culture's prevailing messages with deeper, richer values. It used to be that parents, extended families, and communities passed on their values to the next generation. Now, many children are being raised by the media. TV characters tell them what to buy, how to dress, what to eat, how to talk, what to aspire to, what to love, and what to scorn. Given the power and the pervasiveness of TV and media in our lives, it is not surprising that so many parents feel helpless or have lost faith in their ability to set limits and raise their own children. Rejecting the values promoted by the media takes an enormous amount of effort. It means building a wall around young children and protecting them, for a time, from the culture's prevailing winds. It means educating our children's hearts and minds by fully engaging our own. It means teaching them what *we* love and what *we* value, and clearing space for their own growth—without the influence of the popular culture's conflicting images and messages.

No wonder, then, that turning off the TV, or getting rid of it altogether, can seem like such a radical step. We are a society in the grip of the media, shaped by it and dependent on it for our relaxation, our entertainment, even our education. For many of us, it *is* hard to envision life without the TV; Jake isn't the only kid whose first response would be, "How do you *live*?"

But live we do. I cannot tell anyone to follow in our footsteps, I can only urge you to examine your own family's relationship with television. And I can report that we have found our lives to be challenging, interesting, and full without it. In fact, once the TV screen went dark, the rest of life took on a brighter hue.

Having chosen to eliminate TV from our lives—and discovering that we were all happier without it—it was easy to decide that we could do without video games, computer games, and other electronic entertainment as well. There have been times when we needed to remind our children that the world is full of other good things to do, but rarely. Our boys discovered that for themselves. They don't think less of their friends who disappear inside after school to play Pokémon, nor do they wish they could play, too. They simply aren't very interested. They have other stuff to do. They live.

*A*ll that said, I must admit that the first step in this journey—giving up television—*was* hard at first. I especially hated losing that sacred viewing hour between five and six P.M., the hour when my tired, cranky children were happy to flop down in front of the television while their tired mother got dinner made and on the table. Jack was two at the time, the age at which if he was not watching TV, then I had to be watching *him*. So those first TV-free months did present a challenge. It was easy for me and my husband to give up TV ourselves; it was much harder to give it up as a free and always available baby-sitter for the kids. At the beginning, I had to put a lot of energy into getting us all through the day. I would put out snacks, set up little projects, and then try to dash between whatever I was doing and whatever the boys were doing.

I finally solved the pre-dinner problem by putting Henry, then five, to work and putting Jack into the kitchen sink. We found our way. Henry could set the table, he could peel vegetables, slice a banana, drop walnuts into a salad. And Jack was delighted to take his clothes off and sit in a sink full of warm bubbly water, "washing dishes." It still required more of me, but I got something back, too—happy times with my children. Every day that we made it through without resorting to TV, I felt victorious. We could do it! And over time it did get easier.

Jack graduated from in-sink dishwasher to chief napkin folder. By the time he was five, he knew how to handle a sharp knife and could be entrusted with a pile of potatoes to peel and chop. Sometimes, to help fill the time, I would send both of the boys outside to find treasures for our table—flowers and branches for a centerpiece, rocks and twigs to arrange at each place. As they got older, they made placemats, wrote out menus, set the table. Our dinnertime collaboration meant that both boys grew up knowing a good deal about what goes into a meal and how things are done in our kitchen.

Now they are busy with their own enterprises, and I have long since been relieved of my job as activity director. They don't need any help figuring out what to do with themselves. I still get a hand with dinner sometimes, but many nights I'm alone in the kitchen again, and I find my-self already nostalgic for those years when I had two eager little assistants.

As I think back to the battles my children and I used to have over shows and times and channels and hours in front of the set—and to the vague sense of unease I felt about plopping my young children down in front of the loud, in-sistent sounds and images of television—I realize that the cold turkey approach was the right way for our family. After a few weeks of adjustment, we were weaned. And after that, we never looked back.

In our house, eliminating television cleared a space for the things we really care about. In fact, I don't think it is an exaggeration to say that turning off the TV was the greatest single thing my husband and I have done to foster creativity, imaginative play, and independent thinking in our children. What's more, we realized that we suddenly felt more con-nected to each other and more in touch with ourselves. Somehow we got far more than we gave up. We've found that no TV means

~ More time for music. When Henry doesn't
know what to do with himself, he goes to the
piano or picks up his guitar to pass the time. He
and his dad practice together every day, I've
taken up the recorder, and Jack is the rhythm
section. Many evenings we all sing and play
together.

- More time for reading. We read aloud, we read alone, we read for pleasure and education. In fact, we jump down into books as if they were rabbit holes, passageways into other realms. Everyone in the family has a book going all the time.

- More time for art. There are hours for drawing and coloring and projects. Like music, art is simply part of daily life.

- More time to play.

- More compassion. Television turns us all into jaded voyeurs. When you are bombarded with violence, sex, and catastrophe, you can't help but become desensitized to the images that wash over you. Once we eliminated that daily flood of sensory information from our lives, our own senses seemed heightened. Our children experience life fully and feel it deeply—both its beauty and its sadness.

- More time for each other. No TV has meant that we have all gotten very good at entertaining ourselves; we know how to make our own fun, how to make one another laugh.

- More time to live. We spend our days doing instead of watching; entering into real-life activity instead of disengaging from the world; creating our own images and stories instead of

absorbing manufactured ones. When it's time to
relax, we do so without delivering ourselves
over to the media. We open ourselves to the
moment instead.

*O*nce we see our homes as sanctuaries from a hectic
world, then television begins to feel more and more
like an unsavory intruder, robbing our rooms of life and
meaning, stealing our time, and preying on our souls. When
it comes to TV, less really is more. Or, as my son Henry has
advised me: "Just say that TV fills your head up with other
people's ideas, which means that you don't have as much
room for your own. Also, it's a waste of time." Words of wisdom from a product of the counterculture.

When the TV goes off, life begins.

PLAY

*S*UDDENLY, THE neighborhood is inhab-
ited in the middle of the day. It is the first
Monday of the first week of summer vacation, the sun is
shining, and freedom is in the air. The five children who
convened in our backyard early this morning have just finished bagels and lemonade in the neighbor's garage, and
now they're back, clambering over our swing set like a band
of agile little monkeys. Shoes and socks have been shed—all
the better to take advantage of the soupy mud below—and a
game is taking shape involving an orange traffic cone, two
swings, and a tree branch.

This morning we chalked murals in the driveway, pumped up the bike tires, and took a walk to the creek. But now I've retreated to the porch with a book, and the children are on their own. We have no plans—for today, tomorrow, or the rest of the week. This is their time.

As I spoke with other mothers during the last weeks of school, I discovered that we were all facing summer vacation with the same mixture of anticipation and dread. Knowing that our structured days were about to end, we were busy clearing desks, rearranging work schedules, lining up playdates and child care, and finalizing camp plans. The world as we'd known it since September was about to come to an end, and we were getting ready. Now, as I watch the children lose themselves in their own world of endless summer, I'm glad I took these few days off from my work and that I resisted the temptation to commit our time this week.

So much of the structure that we impose on our children's lives is really intended to make our own lives easier. We don't want to give up *our* freedom, and so we fail to grant our children theirs. As every mother knows, it's easier to sign up for sports camp than to carve out a week to allow your children to follow their own inclinations at home. But children need time that is utterly their own—time to take up residence in their own lives, time to dream through an afternoon, time to play with the kids next door, time to wake up to their own pleasures. Above all, they need some time when we adults aren't calling the shots.

*W*hen I think of my own childhood, I recall step-
ping out the back door on a summer morning,
the grass wet with dew, the whole long day stretching ahead
of me. My parents worked together in an office attached to
our house. They were available for our emergencies and saw
us at lunchtime. Otherwise we were on our own. My
brother and I knew the rules and the boundaries, and we
were expected to honor them. We didn't always, but we
didn't get into serious trouble, either. As a third-grader, I
walked into town for a swimming lesson, then home again.
The rest of the day was my own. I would feed the rabbit in
his cage under the apple tree, then jump on my swing and
pump and sing until my legs were wobbly and I'd belted out
every song in *My Fair Lady*. I might ride my bike to a nearby
dirt pile along with a couple of neighborhood kids. We'd
climb to the top and jump off until the summer heat became too much to bear, and then we'd ride to Dixie's store,
where we'd pool our dimes for orange freeze pops and then
pedal home, one-handed. We'd have races and contests—
who could swing the highest, jump off, and fly the farthest.
We drew lines in the dirt with sticks and kept score. We
played kickball and dodgeball, fought with neighbor kids,
chanted off-color songs. Once, we stole a dented old tea-
kettle from the junkman who lived a few streets away and
whose yard was a veritable mountain of stuff, enticing and

dangerous. As a child in summer, I roamed the neighborhood, tunneled through a huge pile of library books every week, pitched a tent in the yard and slept there night after night, and built a fort in the woods with my brother, where we chewed on strips of tree bark and pretended we were pioneers. . . .

I didn't grow up in the country; I grew up in a typical New England town, where it didn't occur to anyone to plan their children's days or even to keep too close an eye on them when they weren't in school. My childhood seemed—to me then and for many years afterward—completely uneventful. But now, raising children of my own, I consider my childhood rich indeed, for I still hold within me those feelings of freedom and self-reliance, and memories of summer days strung together like beads on a string, all of them mine.

Today, my husband and I are raising our children in a pretty New England suburb. But the landscape of childhood has changed drastically. Ours is a work-driven culture, fueled by the anxieties of two-career families. We overschedule our own days and keep our children yoked to the calendar as well. There are lessons, organized sports, and playdates; videos, computers, and electronic games to fill the hours in between. All too often there is no such thing as "down" time, or even an opportunity for children to expe-

rience the satisfaction of engaging in ordinary activities—
brushing the dog, washing the car with a hose, walking to
town for an ice-cream cone.

Perhaps we adults have lost the fine art of lollygagging,
but at least most of us mastered it as children. We knew
what it was to be bored and to find something on our own
to do; we knew what loneliness felt like; and we discovered
that there was value in being alone sometimes. Left to our
own amusements, we found resources that we didn't know
we had. We learned, as Wordsworth wrote, to see through
"that inward eye that is the bliss of solitude." These were
valuable lessons—and I fear that our own busy, well-
entertained children may not ever have the chance to learn
them. Inventiveness and self-reliance are being scheduled
right out of them.

Yes, it is difficult in our day and age for parents to simply
set children free for the summer. But surely we can manage
to give them a day or a week here and there, during which
we adults fade into the background, erase the schedule, and
simply let them *be*. If we plan all of their days for them, how
will they learn to navigate through the idle shallows of their
own lives, much less seek out and bask in those calm waters?

As this sultry June afternoon wears on, the children find
a baby grasshopper and share him from arm to arm. They
negotiate for turns on the swings and imagine themselves,
by turn, as shipwreck survivors and astronauts flying through
outer space. They shout and sing and whisper among themselves in voices too low for me to hear. Both the jokes and
the disputes that flare up are wholly their own—they don't

need me, and I stay out of it. After a while, their ease with each other is palpable; no agenda here. A child's sense of time and purpose bears no relation to our own, and these kids are in no hurry to get anywhere. To them, a day without a schedule is a day of possibilities. They are on vacation. And all at once, as I glance up from my book to watch a cardinal swoop across the lawn, I realize that I am, too.

RECIPE FOR PRESERVING CHILDREN

Ingredients:

> *1 grass-grown field*
> *several dogs and puppies (if available)*
> *pebbles and sand*
> *½ dozen children or more*
> *1 brook*

Method:

> *Into field, pour children and dogs, allowing to mix well.*
> *Pour brook over pebbles until slightly frothy.*
> *When children are nicely brown, cool in warm bath.*
> *When dry, serve with milk and freshly baked gingerbread.*

Old family recipe

Secret Places

T HE BEST ONES are the ones that children discover on their own, the ones that are imbued, from the very first, with a sense of ownership and mystery; places that no adult would ever think to go, that are hollowed by the shapes of small bodies and furnished by wild nature and rampant imagination. I had several as a child. Indeed, these secret spaces were the real domains of childhood, as fresh and vivid now in my mind's eye as my own girlhood bedroom.

There was the bristly cave, formed by the right-angled intersection of two rows of evergreens in the back corner of my grandparents' suburban yard. Inside, the ground was covered by a fragrant mat of brown pine needles; above, the crowded pines groped and tangled, their branches woven into an impenetrable vaulted arch. Once inside, I was hidden from view, although small breaks in the screen afforded views of the whole house—I could see my grandmother in her chaise longue on the porch, reading her *McCall's* and *Family Circle,* and my grandfather, watering his zucchini with the hose, only a few feet away but ignorant, I was sure, of my surveillance. There was not much else to see, so I spent my hours in this secret place reading secret books, the ones I carried down from my grandparents' hot attic and dusted off, relics from my mother's own childhood: *Black Beauty, Eight Cousins,* and *Heidi Grows Up.*

Back at home, there was a remarkable underground place, a sort of stone cell accessible only by standing on a chair in the basement and hoisting oneself up to and through a small hole in the wall. How my brother and I ever discovered this spot in the first place I don't recall, but its very existence—a bit of unknown territory between the walls of the garage and the basement—was an amazement. We swabbed out the spiders and some of the dirt with a roll of wet paper towels and made big plans. We could live there, under the house, and sneak our food down at night. . . . Although we never did summon the courage to sleep in the hole, as we called it, we did put food by—bags of Fritos and cans of Fresca stolen from the fridge—and we spread an old bedspread over the dirt floor, had two pillows for furnishings, and a flashlight that worked. There was even a window up near the top of one wall, and part of the mystery was our inability to ever figure out, from the outside of the house, where exactly that window was. But inside it allowed for a thin stream of natural light, making the hole just habitable during the day. One autumn afternoon, I took a handful of Concord grapes from our neighbor's abundant arbor and brought them into the hole, where I arranged them in a row on the high stone windowsill, hoping they would turn into raisins. A month later they were ready, shriveled and dusty and brown. I steeled myself there, in my secret place under the house, and ate them one by one, knowing self-sufficiency for the first time.

This spring, my own boys claimed a narrow corridor behind the hemlock trees at the edge of our yard. Backed up against an old stockade fence marking the property line, the trees are a netherland—as far as I'm concerned, the messiest, least attractive area of the whole yard—and when I'm feeling lazy, I throw stones and debris from the garden in there, knowing the stuff will never be seen again. But therein, perhaps, lies the beauty of the place in the children's eyes, for they have found layers of treasure in this secret place. One by one, my gardening tools have disappeared, a couple of them for good, it seems. The boys cleared a space back in there, and then for weeks the yard was empty—all the children were behind the trees, digging. They have found bricks and shards of pottery, coiled springs and a cracked doll's head, a flattened basketball and an old bent spoon, a dog's leash and two bones that lend themselves to ongoing speculation. Over time, a hierarchy emerged in the bushes; rules were made about where the treasures should be stored and who should have access and when. Eventually, as the site yielded fewer discoveries, neighborhood interest waned, and the kids moved on. But now, each of my boys will slip away to the "digging place" when they want to be alone. There is room to stretch out, to sit back against the fence and be shrouded and hidden by the bushes all around, there is a sharp stick to dig with and a pile of treasures to sort through and dream about.

Then, just a week or so ago, the mystery of this place was confirmed all over again. The boys were playing on the swings with two friends. Suddenly the hemlock branches parted behind them, and a little girl with red hair stepped out—a stranger, as they reported to me later, still breathless and eyes wide with wonder. "What are you doing?" she asked.

My sons admitted to me that they had been almost too scared to answer; they thought she might be a ghost, perhaps even the owner of the long-lost doll, returned from the beyond to claim her. "Who are *you*?" Jack finally managed. But the little girl didn't answer, she just turned around and stepped back into the trees.

Such is the province of childhood—questions that float in the air, unburdened by answers; hidden places that are beyond the realm and ken and comprehension of adults. Every child needs such a place, a place that invokes the processes of the imagination and the possibility of transformation. A place that is at once a haven from the adult world and a source of mystery and wonder, a place that a child can discover and shape and lay claim to, simply by virtue of his or her own quiet presence there, and deep observation.

*O*ur contemporary landscape does not always allow for such places. The yard crews are told to clean out the corners, the brush pile is carted off to the dump, the hedges are clipped. Inside, the closets are packed with *stuff*—our possessions spread into every available space, cluttering our homes and crowding our imaginations as well. But surely every yard, every home, has within it some small place that can be left alone—a cupboard under a stairwell, a basement nook, a patch of dirt behind the garage, a clump of ragged bushes—where a child can be allowed to cozy up with a book and a pillow, or to dig in the dirt, or simply to make believe, in peace and dignity.

An urban child ought be allowed the freedom to find and inhabit such a place in a nearby park, a place that is not manicured or even particularly savory, perhaps, but a place that holds forth the possibility of enchantment and meaning. A friend in Manhattan marvels at the ingenuity her son displayed in creating a secret place in their cramped city apartment, claiming the top shelf in his high-ceilinged closet and transforming it into a cozy reading spot. The little boy next door retreats to the uppermost reaches of a pine tree, carrying his necessities in a backpack that he hangs on a branch. His mother holds her breath but leaves him in peace there.

As adults, we furnish our homes and groom our yards and plant our gardens. But long before that, we endow our secret places. The cup, the spoon, the book, the trowel, the polished apple saved for later . . . In choosing these places, and the things that go into them, we learn about who we are and what we love. We learn about the power of place, how to partake of the world's subtleties and secrets, of the human need for sanctuary.

Children need their privacy just as we adults do. In the secret places of childhood, the soul drinks deeply, is refreshed, and flourishes.

WANTſ AND NEEDſ

*I*T WAS A RAINY Saturday, after a week of rainy days, and there was little chance of a reprieve. The children had played on their own all morning; my husband and I had performed the regular weekend chores and errands; now, as we did lunchtime dishes and considered the long afternoon ahead, we all felt at odds with the damp day. Finally the boys decided to color. But no sooner had the crayons and coloring books come out of the closet than Jack decided that he needed a brand-new coloring book, one that had never been touched by human hands or defaced by any wayward Crayola. And he needed it now. Within moments we were engaged in a full-scale debate. There was no reason he could see that I should not get right into the car, drive to town, and buy him a coloring book.

Was it too much to ask? Only a dollar or two! We'd be home in ten minutes! If I would only do this for him, he'd be happy all day! Why was I being so mean?

In fact, I sympathized with my cranky little one. I was itchy and restless, too. I could easily manufacture a few errands downtown, and a trip to the store would be a welcome diversion. I knew just how he felt. The fact is that try as I might to stay centered and focused on what's really important, the world sometimes does win. At times I feel on the losing end of a tug-of-war: on one side, a desire to live simply, without fuss; on the other, the lure of social events, beautiful things to buy, new places to go.

Of course our children experience similar impulses and desires—they yearn for this new toy or those new shoes, for a playdate with this week's best friend, for the awesome breakfast cereal in aisle seven. . . . As mothers with long experience in the art of the plea, the whine, and the bargain, we tend to pick our shots: "You can have the cinnamon raisin bagel, but not the box of Count Chocula. . . ." We know full well that our children are not yet able to distinguish wants from needs. This is why they are such easy prey for advertisers: children want what they see, and the media is one long enticement—to buy, to have, to get.

But many of us are just as confused as our children. We fail to distinguish real needs from wants, and we focus on what we don't have rather than on the abundant gifts that are already ours. When we are consumers, we teach our children that it is good to consume. When we try to resolve conflicts or to buy happiness by spending money, we teach our children to look outside themselves when they feel needy. Unfortunately, many of us feel so overwhelmed by the media's demands for our attention, so inundated by consumer goods, and so buffeted by the pace and complexity of our lives that we have little sense of our own genuine needs from one moment to the next—let alone those of our children.

On the other hand, when we pause long enough to give thanks for the abundance of daily life, when we feel good about what we have right now, we teach our children a valuable lesson: We help them accept that they can't have everything they want, and we reassure them that they *do* have everything they need. This is a concept that I need to reinforce over and over again, both in my own thinking and in day-to-day life with my children. We are living in a consumer society that revolves around instant gratification. We shop for recreation and spend and buy things we don't really need. But unless we want our children to perpetuate this kind of materialism, we must show them another way. And we must give them faith that their real needs—for love, attention, acceptance—will be met.

*I*t was not clear to me exactly what Jack needed right then, although I was reasonably certain that it wasn't a Hercules coloring book. I knew, too, that if I gave in to the want, rather than searching for the need, I might quell his tears but neither of us would be the better for it. I couldn't deliver a lecture against the evils of consumerism to a five-year-old. However, I could lead by example. Right then, I needed to create something positive for us both, without buying anything. I needed to show that we can find joy in something simple and contentment in one another's company. So instead of going to the store, we went back to the closet, where several years' worth of old coloring books are stacked up in various stages of desecration or completion. "I will surprise you by finding a picture for you to color," I said, "and you can surprise me by giving me one. And then we will do them together." He knew then that I wasn't going to change my mind. But he also knew that I was really on his side. I gave him a spiky dinosaur, he gave me a charging knight. And then we sat down together and colored.

Right now, I have everything I need.
When I honor life's gifts with my children,
I teach them abundance and strengthen
their faith that their own needs will be met.

STORIES

I REMEMBER THE NIGHT my children first regarded me as a storyteller. My husband, the boys, and I were driving home after a big Thanksgiving dinner with the extended family. The full moon seemed suspended over the highway to the east, a benevolent fellow traveler gliding along beside us as we journeyed south. The children were too full—from the day's excitement, the holiday feast, encounters with various relatives young and old—to settle down to sleep on the backseat. And soon adult reminiscences of holidays past segued into tales for our sons, then about three and six. My husband told about throwing rocks, as a boy of eleven or so, with his buddy Frog, owner of a brand-new bike. Frog accidentally stepped into the line of fire and took a direct hit on the forehead. "He was covered with blood, and he could hardly stand," my husband recalled, still impressed these many years later by his friend's valor. "But Frog was brave, and he was a true friend. Even with his forehead split open, he said to me, 'It's OK. Just bring my bike home for me, all right?' And then he walked home and they took him to the hospital and put nine stitches in his head." The boys were spellbound. "Keep telling these blood and bone stories!" they urged, bouncing in their seats with the pure joy of it.

I weighed in then with a dramatic account of the day I rode a horse into a wasps' nest, was thrown to the ground and battered and stung in seven places. My husband had a generous store of blood and bone tales—axes bouncing off shinbones, dog bites, slaughtered chickens. And I kept up my end, too, with stories of a full goldfish bowl overturned on a head, broken arms and legs, a cousin's fall through the ice, a great-great-uncle's demise under a tractor wheel, a near-miss with a snake.

We were home too soon. What's more, we had whet an apparently insatiable appetite for stories. But before too many more car rides had passed, I found myself at a loss. My children wanted stories. Not just gory anecdotes, but real stories, stories they could taste and feel and see, stories that would challenge their imaginations, scare them silly, make them laugh, and yet reassure them of the rightness and order of all creation. Stories, certainly, beyond my own childhood recollections. And yet, once I had exhausted my meager store of mishaps and adventures, I had no more stories to tell.

"Make one up," they would press. Too hard, I would

think to myself. As an editor, I know what goes into a story—and I was pretty certain that I was not a storyteller. Surely by the time I could work out a beginning, middle, and an end in my mind; figure out the characters, the moral, and the plot; and begin the tale, the moment for storytelling would be past.

The truth is, I didn't have the nerve to tell stories to my children. I felt I lacked the spontaneity, imagination, and wisdom necessary to make up stories off the cuff, and I was sure I didn't have the time to sit down and work out a full-blown narrative in advance. Besides, with all the beautiful picture books in the world, with all the timeless stories already at our disposal, wouldn't it be enough to read to them instead? And yet, a tradition of sorts had been born as we drove home in the late-autumn darkness under that full moon. It seemed we had entered a new realm of intimacy in the car that night, and we all wanted to be able to return to it at will. The way back in, I knew, was through stories.

Several months later, I joined a storytelling class taught by a therapist and former Waldorf teacher named Nancy Mellon. Each of us, it turned out, was there for the same reason—we yearned to cast magic spells, to spin tales of wonder, to enchant our children with stories—and yet none of us felt quite up to the challenge. By the end of our first morning together, my wise teacher had already given me the key I needed. "Each of us has a storyteller inside," she assured us, "but we may need to find her, and gently wake her up." Locating that storyteller has proved to be a process of learning to see the world through fresh eyes, and learning to put my faith in that unknown part of myself where stories reside.

According to Nancy, our first task as storytellers is to become good listeners and good watchers. And so, at her suggestion, I began to look upon the world itself as the raw material for stories. Suddenly, the moon, the stars, even the raindrops sliding down the windowpanes, all became imbued with life. Something deep within me was aroused. Storytelling, I realized, was not only a way to reach out to my two sons, but also a pathway back into my own intuitive wisdom.

The lessons I learned in this circle of women over the next year were as much about the quality of time, and our need for quiet spaces, as they were about storytelling technique. Real stories take time. They require, first, that we lay our own concerns aside for a while and open ourselves to the present moment. We must make a space for stories, clearing away some of life's clutter so that we can listen with full attention to an inner voice. A candle helps create that ritual space; somehow, a flame invites inspiration while also reminding teller and listener alike of the sacred nature of this work. The internal storyteller is there, but she needs breathing room.

Years ago, parents told stories to children both to entertain them and to teach them about the world's complexities. But we lost the art of storytelling when we lost that sort of open-ended time with our children, the reflecting, wondering, watching time that gives rise to stories. And yet, stories can help our children make sense of life, especially the hard times. When we cultivate the special story mood; when we speak the earth's truth in the form of a story; when we give voice to the hidden relationships between the human world and the natural one, we awaken our children to the connections between all of life. And when we tell a story in a way that invites our children to create their own inner pictures—drawing, perhaps, on images from fairy tales, folklore, and mythology—we introduce them, firsthand, to the collective unconscious that we all share, and to the timeless themes of human life and striving.

Where do our children hear most of their stories today? More often than not, they receive their stories from the media, from huge international corporations who need to make a profit, and who do so by "entertaining" us. These mass-produced commercial stories may capture our children's attention, but they will not stir their senses or open their hearts. Compared to the imaginative riches we can bequeath to our own children, even the most well-intentioned stories and images from television and movies and advertisements seem hollow indeed. As Mary Pipher so aptly put it in her book *The Shelter of Each Other,* stories told by the media "induce children to want good things instead of good lives."

The stories we mothers can tell are different. They are food for the soul, and they nourish us, the storytellers, as well as the listeners. Telling a story is really a way of breathing deeply with our children. Taking that deep breath, exhaling, and putting ourselves at the mercy of something universal, we allow our own voices to become instruments of our souls. To begin, we need only create a "listening" space, tune in to the world around us, and have faith that our own inner storytellers will guide us. Observing the minute particulars of a season, a day, a moment, we discover the stuff that stories are made of: a leaf twirling away on a breeze, a seagull who flies higher than the rest, a worm who has a job to do, a dog on a journey, a stone with a peculiar past, a boy who never wants to go to sleep. . . .

As I began to tell my children such small, impromptu stories, I realized that the world is full of stories telling themselves. I could bring these stories to my sons without knowing where the plot would go or even where we would end up. The stories that seemed most satisfying were often the simplest ones—they made us feel alive and part of things; they fed us and made us happy. The trick, I found, was not to intellectualize or to moralize at all. Better to simply begin right where we were—with a sound in the distance, an ant at our feet, a child's pain or fear, a happy thought, a sad memory. Somehow, the story and I found each other, or so it seemed. And my children, simply by listening, supported my efforts. When I spoke truthfully, I knew they heard me and took my words in at a very deep level. It wasn't even the dramatic action that seemed to bring our stories to life, it was the details—the obsidian glitter of a fox's eye, the haunting scent of woodsmoke in the air, the wiry texture of a gnome's long beard. Suddenly, we were transported. And, as storytelling became a part of our daily life, I realized that, in fact, I did have the time to tell stories, just as we all find time to provide our children with the things they truly need in order to grow and thrive.

*O*ver the last several years, I have stretched myself a bit further. A story at a friend's child's birthday party created a lovely mood of stillness in the moments before cake and ice cream appeared. On Halloween, I donned witch hat and robes. My son summoned the neighborhood children with an eerie song on his recorder, we gathered round a small fire, and I stilled my nerves and began the spooky story I'd prepared. For one very shaky moment, I thought I couldn't pull it off, couldn't keep the story thread from tangling, couldn't hold the attention of this group eager for trick-or-treating to begin. But then it clicked. I looked across the fire at an eight-year-old girl dressed as a blue M&M, her eyes so serious and intent under a shelf of bangs. The storyteller began to speak to her, and the story unspooled around us, casting its spell.

Birthday stories have become another special tradition. They do require time and forethought—time, I suppose, that I could just as easily spend wandering through a shopping mall in search of the perfect gift. Instead, I sit with pen in hand and wait for the perfect story to come. Holding an image of one's child in mind, finding a story to fit a particular moment in time, and practicing that story until it comes to life, seems to me a wonderful way to honor another year of a child's growth. I have adapted stories from other sources, and I have created my own. But a story's origin matters much less than the way it is offered. It is the act of storytelling itself that restores and transforms us. My boys may not remember the gifts they unwrap, but they do remember their birthday stories, for these are gifts of the heart.

Now that they are older, my sons tell stories to each other, and even to their friends. This is real entertainment, especially for their eavesdropping parents. In our family, telling stories is an essential, cherished part of life, and we all have our special characters and ongoing epics, in addition to the short tales. My husband and Jack spent months of bedtimes engaged in the saga of three beloved musketeers: Sadie, a cat with a mile-long tail; a chicken named Bill; and Maurice, a mouse with wings. These nights, their stories are often set in baseball fields and feature extraordinary feats on the mound. (It's hard to tell who enjoys these the most, but my husband reports that the more fun he has spinning these yarns, the more fun Jack has listening.) On long car trips, I continue the episodic adventures of two wandering brothers, Cliff and Mossy. Henry reduces Jack to tears of laughter with his own creation, "the weird little dude," who gets into huge amounts of trouble and talks like a backwoods hillbilly.

*W*hen we tell stories to our children, we reweave our connections to nature, to the spirit world, and to our own sense of holy wonder—connections that are too often broken down by our culture's surfeit of noise and activity. The stories told and retold in our family over the years have become part of us all, and they live on in my sons' memories in vivid, sharp detail. Caught anywhere with ten minutes or an hour to get through, we can turn to stories. The now-familiar mantle of intimacy that we draw around us like a cloak is unique to story time: we turn our eyes upon each other, rather than upon a printed page; the senses quicken; and we are conscious of another presence among us then, "the storyteller," someone more powerful than all of us, yet brought into being by our own intentions. All of this is as magical for me as it is for my sons.

Telling stories is still a challenge for me. This is one aspect of mothering that requires all of my creative faculties, including a willingness to reach deep within, to visualize in precise detail, and to be fully present with my children at the same time. But I also know that whenever I feel that my story well has run dry, it is only because I have not been paying enough attention to my life. And so, for my own sake, as well as for my sons', I stop then, and breathe deeply, and look more closely.

It is early August now, and sometime over the last two nights, the crickets took up their miniature instruments and began the long sonata that announces fall's approach. But underneath the loose rock at the bottom of the front steps lives a small brown cricket who doesn't know the tune; in fact, he really doesn't want summer to end at all. "Perhaps," he thinks to himself . . .

Someplace deep within me, I carry every story
I have ever heard, every story I have ever lived,
every story I will ever need.

ONE-ON-ONE TIME

BEDTIME IS EARLIER than usual in our house these days. At least, it's earlier for my son Henry and me. He's on chapter 12 of *Charlie and the Chocolate Factory,* and I'm halfway through Annie Dillard's *An American Childhood.* The earlier we're both washed and brushed and tucked in under a cool sheet, the more time we have for reading together. Most nights, while my husband and our younger son enjoy their own bedtime story, Henry and I carry mugs of mint tea up the stairs, plump up the pillows, turn on the fan, and close the bedroom door. This is sacred time—he has me all to himself, and it is a highlight of the day for both of us.

Surely it won't go on forever; no doubt by the time school starts again in September we will have fallen into some new variation of the bedtime routine. But for now, this is my way of spending some time alone with my older son, a ritual that was shaped by our shared love of reading and by long summer days that can tire a young body even before dark.

We all know that children need some special one-on-one time with their parents. But sometimes we forget that we parents need this kind of time alone with our children, too. And, unfortunately, when the pace of life speeds up, one-on-one time is often the first thing that gets squeezed out. Our schedules deprive us of each other. Yet when we do that bit of extra juggling required to make a special, separate place for each child, the rewards are well worth the effort.

When Henry was quite young, he was plagued by a series of vague, chronic physical problems. In addition to our endless rounds of visits to doctors' offices, he also received several hours of physical and occupational therapy each week, at different locations. Those appointments devoured huge chunks of my days—but they also ensured that my younger son, Jack—then a toddler—and I had lots of time to spend alone together. While Henry was having his therapy, Jack and I would poke around in the neighborhood. At one location we had a farm to explore, and for a year we made weekly visits to a pig named Zig, a one-legged chicken, horses, and a hutch full of bunnies. Another therapist was located on Main Street in a nearby town. There, hand in hand, Jack and I followed the same route every week, in every kind of weather, stopping always for a chocolate ice-cream cone at Bailey's and to gaze at a Victorian doll-house in a Realtor's window. For Jack, these explorations have long since faded from memory; even Henry can barely recall his weekly rounds to therapists' offices. But I remember them all too well—the struggle to get us to three appointments a week on time, with a toddler in tow. The worry over Henry's prognosis. And, perhaps most of all, those amiable hours with Jack, islands of time that we would not have otherwise had during those harried, difficult years.

Now, some years later, one-on-one time takes different forms. Jack still loves to walk, and a trek through the woods with one parent is his idea of paradise, an opportunity to shed all constraints, to play and pretend, and to share whatever's on his mind. When Henry finished reading his first big chapter book on his own, I had him dismissed from school one day at noon and took him to an Italian restaurant for lunch, marking this important passage in both our lives. Some nights, after dinner, Henry and his dad take a bike ride around the neighborhood. Jack and I like to sit out in the yard in the dark, watching stars wink on and airplanes making their way across the heavens. One stormy night last winter Jack and his dad took the train into the city and had the science museum all to themselves until closing time, as snow piled up nearly two feet deep outside—a father-son adventure that neither of them will ever forget. Back at home, Henry and I built a fire, ordered pizza, and had a picnic on the living room floor.

Other families we know have their own ways to enjoy special parent-child time. One father takes his son to the supermarket every Saturday morning; they do the week's shopping and treat themselves to breakfast *à deux* at a sidewalk café. A friend of mine has a regular swimming date with her oldest daughter at the Y; afterward they dawdle in the locker room and then go out for pastry and tea on the way home. Another friend takes a weekly drawing class with her eleven-year-old daughter. A woman in New York who had just given birth to her second child helped her older son through that transition by leaving the baby with a high school girl for an hour each afternoon while she and her four-year-old took a bus ride through the city. They went with no destination in mind; it was a chance for them to explore, to talk, and, most important, to be alone together, away from the baby. A single mom I know walks the dog late each night with her adolescent son—as long as it's dark, it seems, he's happy to be out with her, and they can talk more freely under the stars than they can in their own living room.

What makes all of these interludes special is the fact that they force us to slow down, to alter the rhythm of our daily lives in order to make time for each other. Given our other obligations and the length of our to-do lists, it is all too easy to forget the good stuff—namely, how much we actually like our own kids as people, how much we enjoy their company, and how important it is for us to have fun together.

Mothers can get so caught up in the caretaking that we may overlook each child's need to be seen as an individual, with unique tastes and temperaments and gifts. But mothering is not just a simple matter of meeting our children's physical needs. We must also strive to meet them at a deeper level, recognizing in each one a special character and fate. It is up to us, as mothers, to see these soul qualities and to honor and protect them. Alone with our children, one on one, we have a chance to see and hear and accept them as they really are, right now, in this moment. We see them not in relation to their siblings, friends, or peers, or as a piece of the larger family puzzle—but as unique individuals, each with a particular destiny to fulfill on this earth. Such recognition is a basic human need.

When we do recognize our children in this way we also invite them to see us more fully, not just as a parent but as another human being, a fellow traveler on life's journey. The family dynamic is set aside in favor of simple companionship. I am amazed by the questions my children ask when we are alone together, by their breathtaking confidences and their acute perceptions of their world. It feels then as if I am being offered a glimpse of their true colors, pure and shining. I see not only who they are, but who they are becoming.

Mothering does not just mean caring for;
it also means caring about—recognizing each
of our children as unique individuals and
cherishing them just as they are.

*J*URRENDER

*A*LL IS NOT SWEETNESS and light at our house. Our younger son, Jack, is heavily armed. It began with a wooden sword. Jack spotted it in a little toy store when he was three, and he pinned his future happiness on it. Real life would not begin for him, he was sure, until that sword was strapped to his hip. Of course, I had long ago staked out my position on toy guns: zero tolerance. So far it had been easy; Henry was a born pacifist. He had, and still has, no interest in things that slice, swat, shoot, fire, explode, or eject. Naively we took full credit for his gentle nature, believing that a peaceful home produces gentle children.

It took Jack to teach us otherwise. When the campaign for the sword began, his fourth birthday was still months away. His father and I told him that boys who wanted swords first had to demonstrate that they were ready for such responsibility. He would have to earn it by keeping his hands off his brother. While Jack struggled to contain his impulses to haul off and whack Henry, I struggled with myself. Was the sword the first step down the slippery slope toward more objectionable weapons? Would Jack be content to be a brave prince slaying imaginary dragons, or would he cast himself in more sinister roles? Could I really deny him the one thing he had ever desperately wanted?

Jack did prove himself worthy of that sword, and his father and I duly presented it to him on his birthday, along with a strict caveat: If the sword ever hit a person, it would disappear forever. The sword is still with us. What's more, in the year that followed, the arsenal did indeed swell, just as I feared it would. It did not take long for our playroom to become the repository for enough pirate swords to arm the neighborhood, a bow and arrow (fashioned by Jack and his dad from sticks and string), a javelin (stick and duct tape), a life-size rifle (made with a sawed-off broomstick, cardboard, a coat hanger, and a roll of packing tape), a slingshot (stick and rubber tubing), and various small toy knives. Our children have bins full of building toys, beautiful art supplies, a cupboard full of games. All of these things are much loved and played with often. But over in the corner, we have an ammo dump.

I'm still not sure what my stance should be. But at a certain point I did realize that in constantly reproving Jack for his interest in toy weapons, and in denying him access to them, I was also rejecting a part of who he is. From the time he began to sit in my lap and listen to stories, he was drawn to tales of conflict, and he was fascinated by the bad guys. At some level, he must also have been able to sense my disapproval, for once, comparing himself with his brother, he said, "I'm bad, because I like pirates and guns." It occurred to me then that perhaps I wasn't doing him any favors with my high-minded moralizing and that we needed to explore a different path. I also had to face the fact that the more I insisted that we would not have toy weapons of any kind, the more obsessed with them Jack became. Perhaps there was a lesson for me here. Perhaps I needed to surrender.

Just as I had feared, once my guard came down, the munitions multiplied rapidly. Jack was in heaven, drawing intricate colored pictures of rifles; disappearing into the basement for hours with his father to tinker with bits of wood and string; always thinking, it seemed, of the next thing he simply had to have—a musket like Adam's; a foam-dart gun like the neighbor's; a rocket launcher like the one he saw at a birthday party. Finally, though, he zeroed in on the idea of a real cap gun. My brother—the kindest, least confrontational man I know, who nevertheless fired off a few thousand rounds of caps as a kid—was only too happy to oblige.

The cap guns he gave Jack for his fifth birthday were the real thing: ivory handles, metal barrels, a chamber for a big old-fashioned roll of one hundred caps. Jack was thrilled. I felt that I had failed as a mother.

To my surprise, though, Jack had no interest in loading

those guns right away. He carried them around for a while, decked himself out in full cowboy regalia, practiced a quick draw and a snarl to go with it—but never mentioned the caps. Then one night, while I was making dinner a few weeks later, he came into the kitchen and asked if we could go outside and shoot his cap gun. "Sure," I said. I put in the roll of caps and we stepped out into the yard. "You shoot it first," he said. I held my arm straight out and fired. The sound cracked through the night, and a satisfying spiral of smoke rose into the air. But when I handed the gun to Jack, he shook his head.

"Try a little gunplay, Mom," he suggested. I gave it a fancy whirl on my trigger finger, snapped the gun back into my hand, and fired again, three quick ones. "You're a pretty good shot, Mom," Jack said approvingly. And then, "I don't really like the smell of that smoke." He didn't want to shoot the gun himself, but he wanted me to fire off a few more rounds. For a moment there, the pacifist mom of today came face-to-face with the little girl of long ago who loved wild games of cowboys and Indians herself. Bam! Bam! Bam! Satisfied, Jack shoved the gun back into his holster, took my hand, and we went inside for supper.

*J*on Kabat-Zinn, a meditation teacher who writes about mindful parenting, suggests that we think of our children as Zen masters housed in small bodies, who come into our lives to push at all of our fixed ideas. They are our best teachers, he says, and one way or another they will teach us whatever hard lessons we most need to learn. I still don't feel completely comfortable about backing down from my position on toy guns, nor am I certain it was the right thing to do. But I suspect that I did more for Jack, and more for our relationship in the long run, by lightening up a little bit and by remembering how it felt to be a kid myself. Better that I should fire a few caps into a chilly December night than deliver yet another lecture on the evils of guns and violence. My son has a sweet nature and a tender heart, and I simply had to put my faith in his innate goodness— even while allowing him the space he needed to play his way through an important stage of his development.

Since then, his fascination with all these weapons has waned considerably. Jack finally did shoot his cap guns one day a month or two later, but when one broke and was consigned to the trash can, he didn't seem to mind seeing it go. The pirate swords haven't been touched for months, and these days his creative energy goes into drawing colored snowflakes and shooting baskets. If anything, we are closer now to living in a completely demilitarized zone than we have been for two years. Jack's moved on, and so have I.

*T*his is one thing motherhood has taught me: Living according to my values does not necessarily mean being rigid in my convictions about what's "right." Sometimes our children's needs do not coincide neatly with our own beliefs. And therein lies a challenge. Do I try to control every aspect of our family environment, or do I allow others to help shape it, too? Do I always enforce the rules, or do I sometimes step aside and trust my children to find their own way? Surrendering is always an act of faith, and letting go is never easy.

Just a few days ago, I wrote about reading with Henry and how I cherished our quiet time together before sleep on these summer nights. Last night Henry had a "reading date" with his pal across the street. He was washed and in PJs when he skipped over there, barefoot, his book under his arm. The two little boys read on the back porch until bed-time; afterward Henry announced, "We're going to read to-gether like that every night." Good-bye, old ritual; hello, new. . . . And therein lies another lesson in surrender.

When we try to hold on tight to anything, we find our-selves grasping at air; when we struggle to possess—a per-son, a time, a way of doing or being—the very thing we seek slips away. So it is with my most treasured rituals. The moment I try to carve them in stone or to institutionalize them in any way, they seem to vanish before my eyes. Then, rather than try to force the family back into old vessels that no longer fit, I must shape new ones. As soon as something fails to work for us, it is time to let go and create something fresh. This kind of surrender is not easy, either—but neces-sary if we are to continue growing together as a family.

There is another kind of surrender involved in being able to trust that your children and partner can manage for a time without you. For some of us, this letting go is hardest of all—if a thing is going to be done, we want it done our way. But our own desire for control can become a prison. I know a mother who was so critical of her husband's inept handling of their newborn son that he gave up trying to help, thereby depriving her of some much needed support and their son of an early bonding experience with his father. A friend refused her daughter's request to sleep over at her best friend's home, because she didn't approve of the family's diet; she wanted her daughter to eat *her* food. Another friend, whose husband travels frequently for his job, refused for years to accompany him on one of his trips because she would not leave her children overnight; in the end, her inflexibility almost cost them their marriage.

It is good for us mothers to remember that, while we may be irreplaceable, we are not indispensable. Life will go on without us—it will just go on somewhat differently. Last winter, my husband took care of our sons while I spent a week in Florida with my mother. He took them ice-skating every day and didn't wash their hair once; they ate pizza, stayed up late, and let the cat drink from their cereal bowls at breakfast. They had fun, and so did I—but first I had to let go.

*P*erhaps my sweetest lesson in surrender occurred on a day when I was too sick with the flu to do anything *but* let go. My husband was at work; I was in bed with a raw throat and a fever; the boys, then five and eight, had a whole day to fill. Outside, a freezing rain encased the world in ice. For a long time, I dozed and left the kids to their own pursuits. At some point, Henry and Jack came in and whispered in my ear that they were going to bake cookies for me. Although both boys had often helped with our baking projects, they had never flown solo in the kitchen before. Henry reminded me that he could read a recipe. Jack said he was content to be "second boss." And I was sick enough to agree to almost anything that didn't threaten great bodily harm to any of us.

I mustered the strength to exact just three promises: that they not fight with each other, that they call me to take the cookies out of the oven, and that they clean up. And so they were off, excitement running high. Over the next hour or so, tuning in with half an ear, I was conscious of the busy hum down below, the earnest discussions, the sounds of chairs being dragged across the floor. Part of me couldn't believe that I was allowing my two small sons sovereignty in my kitchen; the other part of me was praying for this peaceful interlude to last as long as possible.

At last, the scent of baking cookies wafted up the stairs. I could hear the cleaning crew take up their tools down below. The water ran for a long time. So did the vacuum. And then the buzzer went off and it was time for me to make the great descent into—what? When I walked into the kitchen, I saw my boys there, aprons tied around their waists, eyes shining with pride. Things weren't perfect or spotless, but their effort in that direction was everywhere apparent. Henry had been stymied in his dishwashing by the last of the sticky cookie dough on the bowl, and they hadn't quite managed to do away with all traces of spilled flour—but by and large things looked amazingly good. They had squeezed all of their cookies onto one baking sheet and were delighted to discover that, as a result, they had baked one enormous chocolate-chip cookie. Magic! I spent five minutes wiping down the counters and carried a little hunk of cookie back to bed.

Our faith in one another deepened on that day. The boys wore my trust in them like a mantle—they were shining knights in the kitchen, handling tools and fire with respect. Seeing what they were capable of, I suddenly had to regard them in a new light. In surrendering, I gave them a space to grow up into, and that is just what they did.

Tonight, Henry will read with his friend until bedtime. And I have promised Jack that we will have a special story time together. Something surrendered, something gained.

> *In surrender, I clear a space in which*
> *something new can grow. I place my faith*
> *in something larger than me. I trust.*

POSTSCRIPT

There is a sequel to my story about Jack and his cap guns. A year after I wrote the words above, two teenage boys opened fire on their classmates in Littleton, Colorado. In the days and weeks that followed the shooting, parents and educators across the country searched for answers to the question that haunted us all: How could this happen?

I sense that many of us feel a deep-seated ambivalence about the violence in our society. We decry violence with words, yet we accept it in our lives, in the form of toys, movies, television shows, action figures, computer games. Suddenly, though, in the wake of those killings committed by two young boys, I felt I could afford my own ambivalence no longer. It was simply no longer possible for me to rationalize to myself the presence of guns in my children's toy chest. But it was not until I sat in church a couple of Sundays later, listening to our minister struggle with his own response to the Littleton tragedy, that I found the will to act. "The endemic violence in our culture will be transformed most effectively not by isolated, heroic actions on the part of a few (which is simplistically satisfying)," he said, "but by consistent, repeated, ongoing activity by all of us (which, though personally demanding, is, in the end, far more heroic)."

How, I wondered, could I do my part? But of course, I already had my answer. I could begin in my own home, with my own two sons, by renewing my own commitment to peace. Jack was six and a half now, grown up enough, I thought, to begin to consider his own choices and to make his own commitments. Perhaps he was ready to lay down arms himself. Our sons had seen none of the images of Littleton, had heard nothing of the shootings. Without television and media, they are spared most of the grim news that saturates our airwaves and newspapers each day. That afternoon, Jack and I took a walk. Choosing my words carefully, I explained why I had become uncomfortable with our stash of toy weapons. Jack listened intently, without saying a word. When I asked if he would agree to get rid of the remaining guns in our house, he didn't hesitate. They could go. "But," he said thoughtfully, "I'd just like to keep that one that Dad and I made out of the broomstick and cardboard. We worked so hard on that, and it's really special to me. I won't ever play with it, just keep it."

The next day, it was Jack who gathered up the weapons and stuffed them into a trash bag. Then, as we'd agreed, we made a special trip to the toy store to buy a very cool yo-yo. When Jack spotted the special holster that holds your yo-yo on your belt, I said yes to that, too.

So Jack learned a lesson in surrender himself and what it means to take a stand, even in a small way, for something you believe in. I was proud of both of us that day. We planted a tiny seed for peace.

BREATHING

YEARS FROM NOW, when I recall summer nights from my boys' childhoods, I am sure that one recurring image will be the two of them at dusk, running barefoot through the grass, pell-mell, around our house. After each full circle, they stop before us and place our palms over their pounding hearts. For them, the inner workings of their own bodies offer an endless source of awe and mystery. We stand there together, hands to hearts, as their pulses slowly return to normal. Then they are off again, flying, exhilarated, reveling in their discoveries of air and speed and strength, the joy of physical experience.

We began this ritual a couple of years ago, as a means of running off excess energy before bedtime; it was our children who transformed it into a celebration of life—indeed, into a kind of holy rite. Sometimes they take off all their clothes and run naked. One unseasonably warm Easter evening, Jack shed his holiday finery one article at a time as he circled the house over and over again, whooping with glee, a tiny sprite darting by us under a pale spring moon. Often a neighbor child or two will join in for a few laps; then they will pair off, run in opposite directions, turn up the heat. Always, though, we must bear witness to the real marvel, the throbbing hearts, testaments to the life and power contained within their bodies. Finally, exhausted, the boys flop to the ground, panting and sweaty and thrilled with themselves.

For many adults undertaking a spiritual practice for the first time, it feels strange, at first, to focus on breathing. We are asked to clear our minds of all other thoughts and to simply pay attention to our own breath, inhaling and exhaling slowly and deliberately. The simplest form of meditation, this kind of breathing can be an effective way to begin to bring one's body, mind, and spirit into harmony. I was surprised to find how readily my children are able to focus on their breath—but perhaps it is because they are still so attuned to their bodies and so willing to give themselves over to pure physical sensation. Their own heartbeats inspire them to reverence; little wonder, then, that they also seem to know, intuitively, that their breath is worthy of the same careful attention.

Jack, with a tendency to shout first and think later, is learning to take ten long, deep breaths with me before reacting to a difficult situation. We hold hands and take those breaths slowly, in unison, gazing right into each other's eyes. Usually the hurt and anger has melted away by the time we're done. Often, when I feel ready to lose my own temper, I take slow, deep breaths deliberately, so that my children can see exactly what I am doing. They know then that I am angry, and they also know that I am working to keep my temper under control.

Over the years I have tried all sorts of solutions to the inevitable sibling battles, including forced separations, time-outs, hugs and kisses, and, at times, shouting at the top of my lungs. Breathing together works best. Now, before I will listen to either side of the story, before the argument escalates further, before I take any action at all to settle a dispute, we breathe together. I kneel down and take one child in each arm. We look into one another's faces, we breathe long and slow and deep, we count to ten or twenty. In the process, we always seem to find in our hearts a scrap of forbearance, a shred of forgiveness—and that is the beginning of the road back to harmony.

*B*reathing is truly the essence of life, the link between our own bodies and the world around us. In Eastern traditions, one's breath is seen as the conduit between human life and the universal energy of the cosmos. Each time we pause to breathe deeply with our children, we are affirming their life forces and celebrating our miraculous existence on the planet in this place and time. When I say to my boys, "Let's take a deep breath," I am guiding them into a safe haven, a place where they can release their pain and anger and come back to center again.

In time and with practice, children can learn to invoke this strategy themselves. In our family it has proven particularly valuable as a means of reforging loving connections in times of stress. Jack is still prone to tantrums, outbursts that frighten him and wreak havoc on the rest of us as well. Sitting with him in his room during these emotional hurricanes, riding them out together, I came to realize that the most frightening aspect for him is the sensation of being out of control. At these times he is at the mercy of his own gale-force emotions, battered, pounded, and flattened by the storm. Now, when he falls apart, I watch for a particular moment when I can see that he might be able to come back to himself—and then we breathe together, finding a rhythm that calms and soothes, that reconnects us, soul to soul.

As we venture back to resume our day, I am reminded

that, just as simple pleasures offer the most satisfaction, so too do simple solutions often prove the most effective. There is the unparalleled rapture of running until it feels as though one's heart will burst. And there is the solace of coming home to one's own breath when all else seems dark and uncertain. How readily our children embrace these humble lessons; how long it takes for many of us adults to relearn them!

Breathing in I calm my body.
Breathing out I smile.
Dwelling in the present moment
I know this is a wonderful moment.

—THICH NHAT HANH, *Being Peace*

Healing

My OLDER SON is undone by a hangnail. My younger falls apart over a bumped shin during a late-afternoon soccer game in the yard. A friend's nine-year-old daughter complains each night of back pain that keeps her awake. Suddenly, the shoes that felt fine yesterday pinch unbearably today. Bumps and bruises, aches and pains—they are the inevitable, minor irritations of childhood, as universal as bad dreams and runny noses. We are inclined to dispense a quick hug and a reassuring word, and to carry on.

But sometimes our children are really asking for more from us than a perfunctory response, and that is when we must minister not only to the skinned knee, but to an inner need as well. It does no good to advise a weeping child that the pain will go away on its own. We are mothers, after all, and it is our job to *do* something. And so I created the "hurt basket," a treasure chest of magical lotions, potions, and healing aids. The wicker basket, stored high on a bathroom shelf, invokes a ritual—it means that time will be taken to ease a pain, that I care, that I will do my best to bring comfort. The contents of the basket change with the season; soothing throat lozenges in winter, an "itch eraser" for summer's mosquito bites. . . . But in general we are not without peppermint foot lotion, arnica gel, witch hazel, calamine lotion (the dramatic pink color is a most effective distraction from pesky itches and a good reminder not to scratch), Weleda Wound-Care and Betadine ointment for cuts, Ben-Gay for mysterious aches and pains, aloe for burns, and last, but not least, a truly impressive array of Band-Aids—glow-in-the-dark Band-Aids, tattoo Band-Aids, animal Band-Aids, smiley faces and ferocious ones, Day-Glo colors, and zebra skins. To an adult, a Band-Aid may be nothing but a sticky plastic strip; but to a child it is a badge of honor, imbued with magical healing properties. Be grateful, and stock up.

When my son dissolves into tears twenty minutes before dinner over a bumped shin that would not even slow him down at nine in the morning, I know how he feels—tired, hungry, cranky, an accident waiting to happen. It is no good, then, to examine that fair, unbroken skin and pronounce him "fine." He needs tending. I scoop him up and carry him inside, set him on the counter, and apply a cool damp cloth to his leg. Gently pat it dry. Squeeze a bit of arnica gel on the sore spot and rub it in. A Band-Aid, too, which he carefully selects. Then a washcloth for his tear-streaked face, a drink of water, a snuggle, and a kiss. . . . The five minutes of nurturing is well spent, for afterward he is fortified, strong again, able to make it through till dinner is on the table. His leg, of course, was fine to begin with; it was his soul that needed a healing moment.

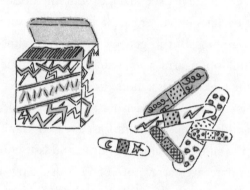

*W*hen we minister to our children with love and care, we teach them to care for others in return. Through our own loving example, we show the healing way, opening their hearts to the needs of those around them. This was brought home to me last Christmas Eve, when Jack, in a moment of careless exuberance, jumped up and banged my mouth with the top of his head, leaving me with a bleeding split lip that quickly swelled to twice its normal size. His eyes brimming with tears of remorse, Jack brought me ice from the freezer wrapped in a soft cloth, and a glass of water. Throughout the rest of the evening he stayed in my lap, kissing my cheek and holding my hand, not only shouldering the responsibility for my injury, but doing all in his power to bring me comfort, too. I had a fat lip, but I also had all the love I could want, and I went to bed that night grateful for my early Christmas present—my five-year-old son's gentle touch and generous heart.

The day will come, of course, when our small ministrations are no longer enough to ease our children's pains, but until then, we can stock their emotional larders with a bounty of love and tenderness, precious stores for the future.

When I comfort my children with love and care,
I teach them compassion.

LISTENING

*I*N ORDER TO listen, we must first be quiet. I can tell my children to stop talking and hope for cooperation, or I can invite them to listen—and know that they will be delighted to tune in to the world's music. I have seen a class of thirty second-graders walk through the woods in companionable silence, each one listening to the sound of wind in the leaves and the crunch of pine needles underfoot. The other day, Jack and I lay absolutely still on the back lawn, trying to hear the autumn leaves falling.

In this noisy world of ours, there are times when the only way to be heard at all is to shout above the din. We scream for attention, one voice raised above the multitudes, and hope our children hear us. And the children themselves clamor, squeal, and yell—they are exuberant creatures, bursting with sound and energy. But within each child there is also an innate talent for listening that deserves to be honored and encouraged.

The simple words "once upon a time" still cast a magic spell, drawing children into the hushed intimacy of story time. Sometimes we must listen in order to discern the truth of a moment. Or we may choose to hold our tongues in order to listen to another's point of view, instead of lashing out in anger. We may simply sit, waiting and listening to whatever lies within.

Certainly we have all strained to hear the voice of our own intuition—a faint murmur, all too easily drowned out. Thus we learn that we need a quiet space in which to listen, if we are to discern the intimations of our own souls. Finding the way to that quiet listening space is a part of many spiritual traditions—we may seek it through prayer, by meditation, or in communion with nature. And we may discover that it takes great courage and determination to listen and to wait for truth to emerge. As anyone who has ever practiced meditation knows, it is a real challenge even to slow down long enough to listen to the sound of one's own breath. Listening involves making a choice—right now, for just a moment—to stop dead in your tracks. To stop moving, to stop talking, to stop making noise. As Madeleine L'Engle has said, "When I am constantly running, there is no time for being. When there is no time for being, there is no time for listening."

We give our children a great gift when we help them to tune in to the muted sounds of earth and sky, of soul and spirit. It is a joyful lesson, offered in the spirit of play, even as they learn the discipline of listening. All we need to do is lead them into quiet moments and allow them to open their ears.

A friend who meditates each day lets his young child lay her head in his lap and listen to him breathing, lovingly folding her presence into his practice. (My own boys like to put their heads on their dad's stomach—the fantastic gurgles and gushes of his digestive system are a continuing source of delight and wonder.) Sometimes I ring a chime and listen with my children until the very last ripple of sound vanishes into nothingness. A favorite seashell is a vessel for the eternal music of the sea. There is nothing special about listening; the beauty of it is that it can be done anywhere, at any time.

Find a dry spot to sit with your child on a sunny winter day and listen to the snow melt—you will both be astonished at the subtle symphony of sound. Sit in the car together, before you turn the key in the ignition, and listen to rain fall on the roof. Ask your children to listen to the world around them for two or three minutes—and then compare impressions of what each of you heard. Listen to a cat purr, and notice all the variations in tone and tempo. Listen to an airplane as it makes its way across your sky, until it is out of sight and, finally, out of earshot. Listen to a bee as it takes nectar from a flower. We can all find a moment in every day for listening, a moment in which we gather our children close, open our ears, and luxuriate in the sounds of our world, wherever we may be.

On summer nights, when our upstairs windows are flung open and the children's bedtime arrives before full darkness, we often turn off the lights and lie on the bed together, while the birds are saying good night. The violet shadows deepen, the children's breathing slows as the cares of the day drift away, and we listen. When the last bird has had its last word, and all is still, it is time for us to whisper our own good-nights. Sometimes we lie silent for a long time, half-asleep, perhaps, but still listening, waiting for one final trill, the night's mysterious, conclusive solo. Troo loo, troo loo, good night.

Listening, we open ourselves to the soul's
true voice and to the world's music.

NATURE

I CANNOT FIND THE breakfast tree now. The woods where I roamed as a child have become checkered with house lots, the wild places mostly vanished. The breakfast tree was nothing special, really, just a tree near the path behind my house, one that happened to have enough low-slung branches so that I could climb it easily, without fear. But in my memory, this kindly tree is a treasured friend, still alive in my imagination. The breakfast tree got its name on the summer morning that my mother agreed to get up early with me, pack us a picnic, and join me for breakfast up among the boughs.

Looking back, I find it amazing that my mother and I actually did this at all—she has never liked heights, for one thing, and she wasn't really the sort of mother one would expect to find up in a tree, sipping orange juice, at six-thirty in the morning. Yet she did agree to my plan, prepared our breakfast basket, and headed out to the woods with me. I remember that we were very pleased with ourselves, sitting up there on our perch while the forest came to life around us, and that we promised to make a regular morning pilgrimage to have breakfast in our tree.

We never did do it again. But perhaps once was enough after all, for we both recall the magic of that morning, how lovely it was. Over the years, I've come to think of the breakfast tree as a symbol of my childhood and of what I loved most about being a child—the kind of casual, daily intimacy with nature that was simply a way of life, a way of life that I took wholly for granted then and for which I am deeply grateful now. I suspect that the breakfast tree symbolized something for my mother, too—it was a point of entry into my child's world, a place where a busy mother and a little girl once took in the world's wonders together, in a spirit of shared adventure and discovery.

I thought of the breakfast tree—and of how much I cherish the thirty-year-old memory of a single happy hour there—the other night when my own two sons invited me to sleep out in the tent they had set up in the backyard. They know full well, as I once knew in my own bones, that nature is not something we need to go in search of, but, rather, something that awaits us all on the other side of our own back doors. "You will love it, Mom!" they promised.

As a matter of fact, I had been looking forward to a cool shower, my own soft bed, a new magazine, and my husband. But looking into their eager eyes, I remembered the breakfast tree and the rare pleasure of my own mother's companionship. So I said yes, I *would* love it.

Out we went, lugging our flashlight, water bottle, pillows, and a stack of Tin Tin comics to the campsite—all of twenty yards from the back steps. Zipped in, our gear arranged around us, we regarded the night. A lone firefly danced a luminous solo through the darkness. The boughs of the pine tree rustled softly above our tent, whispering, "Hush." Branches hung down low around the door flap, too, a fringed black canopy. Seen from the ground up, our own dark house seemed strangely sinister, a looming, gothic silhouette. The moon, just a day away from full, rose ripe as a melon, surrounded by dim stars. Far away a dog howled. We inhaled the fragrant, cooling air and luxuriated there in the glory of a summer night. To think—it had been right here within our reach all the time, and here we were at last, drinking it in. "Let's do this every night," they proposed. "We could probably live out here all summer," Henry murmured. Finally, curled against me like puppies, my sons drifted off to sleep, oblivious of the hard ground, the slippery sleeping bags, the single mosquito that had slipped in with us and was feasting now on sweet boy flesh. Less innocent, I lay awake for a long time. Knowing that we wouldn't be here every night, I also knew that we were blessed for now, and I wanted to make it last.

I think we parents have come to think of nature as something we need to *teach* our children, something we are meant to provide as a part of their well-rounded education, like music lessons and team sports. My husband and I have dutifully taken our children on a whale watch, to the planetarium, up and down small mountains, and to the natural history museum; we've even sent them off to a week of farm camp for close encounters with cows and pigs and chickens.

Yet I've come to realize that a few small, familiar places have made far deeper impressions on my children than all of the whales and panoramic views and rain forest exhibits we could ever offer. The encounters with nature that mean the most to them are those that happen without any agenda at all, beyond going forth to see what's out there. My sons' exuberance and curiosity carry them into an enchanted world full of wonder and possibility, into tide pools and treetops, through mud puddles and into mossy clearings, down into holes and up over rocks.

Over and over again, my children open my eyes to places and pleasures I might otherwise have missed altogether. I once asked Henry to name his favorite spot in the world, half expecting he would choose the Chinese buffet at the Far East Cafe. I was way off; his favorite place, he told me without hesitation, is a field of tall grass at his grandmother's house, a field I scarcely knew existed. One night, as I tucked Jack into bed, he began to paint for me a word picture of the landscape behind his school. Astonished, I listened as he described, in intimate detail, the rocks and trees and paths that he and his classmates had laid claim to. To me it is a patch of pretty conservation land; to them it is a whole world called Golden Woods, marked by the hyena trail, the pine-needle place, the tangled trees, the rock quarry, the tepees, muddy land, and the secret hideout. During his last week of kindergarten, Jack made a booklet in which he painstakingly drew and colored pictures of all these places—because, he said, he wanted to remember them all his life. This, I realize now, was the best kindergarten curriculum he could have had—a year of outdoor mornings. And the little book he made sums up the invaluable lessons the earth provided—direct, meaningful experiences in nature that have fed his soul for life and enlivened his imagination.

Pulling me out to the tent the other night, my sons reminded me once again that even our familiar backyards can surprise us. In fact, children and adults alike can discover the same place over and over again, simply by taking a closer look. We don't need to climb mountains or sail over seas to meet nature; we need only join our children, down on our hands and knees, and watch the intimate movements of a small creature going about its business.

It is so easy in our culture to lose touch with the natural world altogether. We believe we don't have time for nature, and so we ignore our own primal hunger for earth and water and sky. Modern life calls us away from nature's rhythms, away from the kind of observation and interaction with the natural world that can quiet a troubled mind, restore a sense of well-being, and renew our connections with all life. We spend our days inside instead, yoked to some other rhythm, bathed in artificial light, breathing recycled air, surrounded by man-made materials—concrete, glass, and plastic. More and more, our children are spending their days in such environments, too—in brightly colored classrooms, in structured after-school programs, and on man-made playgrounds and athletic fields that offer little in the way of natural beauty. Little wonder, then, that so many of us suffer from a vague sense that something important is missing from our lives or that our children are growing up without a comfortable, enduring, firsthand relationship with the land. Perhaps they don't even know what they are missing, for they cannot yearn for something they have never known themselves.

As the nature writer Robert Michael Pyle has observed, many children today suffer from what he calls "the extinction of experience." Unlike children of earlier generations, they simply do not have the kind of direct, frequent contact with the earth and its creatures that result in a passionate, lasting relationship with the natural world. Our children, he points out, may have "politically correct" responses to whales, global warming, pollution, and rain forests; they are well versed in the major environmental issues—but far less grounded in their own visceral, firsthand experiences. Their actual physical contact and intimacy with nature is fading away. It is not enough, then, to teach our children *about* nature; we must allow our children to grow up *in* nature.

*A*ny relationship requires time, lots of it. If a child is to truly love the natural world, to experience its beauty and truth and power at a spiritual level, he or she must first spend time in natural places. In the end, those who will make a real difference in our world—those who will grow up with the confidence and the imagination to help save the earth—will be those who know it well and love it deeply.

So we parents do have an important role to play. We can take our children with us and head out the door. We can go along as they clamber over rocks, splash through streams, dig in the dirt. We can hunt for hermit crabs, follow caterpillars, count stars. We can take them out of doors and turn them loose, and allow them to find sanctuary in their own special places. We can muse and wonder with them, gather stones and shells and seed pods, celebrate the seasons, and embrace all kinds of weather.

And here is the wonderful secret: Our children offer us an opportunity to rediscover the marvels of nature for ourselves. You don't need any special knowledge, any equipment, or even much of a plan. You don't need to be a naturalist or a teacher. In fact, you don't need to identify a single bird or flower or constellation. All you need is a willingness to go, to look, and to drink in the mystery and beauty of the world before your eyes. I used to wish I had more knowledge to impart, a better foundation in the earth sciences, so that I could explain the world to my children instead of simply experiencing it with them. Certainly our outings gave rise to more questions than answers. But as we watched and wondered together, I came to suspect that our shared experience was probably more valuable to my children than any education I could provide. In time, they will acquire knowledge, too—but first they need the time and space to develop an emotional connection with the land, forging their own relationships with plants and animals, earth and sky. "It is not half so important to know as to feel," naturalist Rachel Carson reminds us in her time-honored classic, *The Sense of Wonder.* And she advises, "If a child is to keep his inborn sense of wonder, he needs the companionship of at least one adult who can share it, rediscovering with him the joy, excitement, and mystery of the world we live in."

When we open ourselves to nature, when we explore the world around us with our feelings and emotions rather than our intellects, we engage all our senses—and we invite our children to do the same. So for now, at least, I try to resist the impulse to explain too much, for all those words can keep us from making deeper observations. I even quell the voice that wants to say, "Don't fall," or, "You'll get soaked," or, "Come in out of the cold." Experience includes extremes, and children need to feel them, need to test their own limits. On a pale gray day last April, I did not protest when my boys decided to take a wade through a nearby creek with their rain boots on. I didn't scold when Jack "accidentally" slipped and sat down smack in the middle of the icy water. And I even kept my mouth shut when his older brother immediately followed suit, splashing down beside him. My restraint was rewarded by their joy. They rose, dripping and triumphant, shouting, "We had the first swim of the year!" And then they ran for home, hollering for the thrill of it and to keep from weeping with cold. "Well," Henry proclaimed cheerfully as they headed inside for dry clothes, "I guess that was enough nature for one day!"

The world, seen through the eyes of a child, is a delicious, irresistible place. And, for the moment, anyway, I am the lucky adult companion of two little boys, my own sense of wonder renewed each time we step out the door and look around us.

> *A child who is allowed to fully experience the*
> *beauty and power of nature receives a gift for life,*
> *a gift that will deepen and grow in meaning*
> *over all the years to come.*

Enchantment

*There is nothing you can do if you have a Brownie
in the house, except to leave him a bowl of hot porridge
every night by the fire, with plenty of milk in it and
a long-handled spoon to sup with.*

—MOLLIE HUNTER, "THE BROWNIE"

IS THERE A BROWNIE in your house?
If there is, you will never catch sight of him,
but you will soon feel certain that he is there. No one knows
what a brownie does by day, but he is surely up all night,
finding missing puzzle pieces, yesterday's lost homework,
and Dad's reading glasses. If you're lucky, he will restore order
to a cluttered room, put the toys back on their shelves, and
wipe the muddy footprints from the floor. He may even slip

into your kitchen in darkest night and set your breakfast table, cut a ripe cantaloupe into juicy chunks for hungry children to find in the morning, or slip a special treat into a waiting backpack. As you will surely agree, a brownie is a most welcome member in any family. All he asks in return for his hard work is to be well fed and to be left alone! If he is treated with respect by the children of the house, he will repay their small kindnesses many times in return.

Henry's wise kindergarten teacher cultivated a rich relationship with a brownie (she called him a "broonie") in her classroom. The children worked very hard at cleanup time, so that the broonie would not have to do all the work himself, and before they went out to play they often left him a little snack in a basket on the table. Magically, when they returned from their outdoor adventures, the classroom would once again be orderly and sparkling, the small offering vanished. Soon the children could detect the hand of the broonie everywhere—a toy broken one day would be mysteriously mended the next; a lovely new stone or shell would be discovered on the nature table; a lost treasure would suddenly reappear, in its rightful place. Very subtly, the atmosphere of the classroom became infused with a gentle magic. One day, Henry wondered if, just perhaps, we might be lucky enough to have a brownie at our house. We decided to find out, and that night he left a cookie and a glass of milk on the kitchen table. The fact that nothing but crumbs remained the next morning was proof enough for him, and we thereupon began to see all sorts of evidence of the brownie's secret existence. Later we discovered Mollie Hunter's eerie tale "The Brownie," describing one determined brownie's efforts to maintain residence in an Irish farmhouse.

When Henry was in second grade, and Jack had just been introduced to the broonie in his own kindergarten class, my husband and I discovered to just what an extent this stealthy sprite had captured both boys' imaginations. They had been working for hours on a complicated K'Nex model, poring over the instruction manual and trying to piece together a solar-powered merry-go-round with a thousand parts. But shortly before bedtime, they hit the wall. The directions didn't make sense; nothing worked; and they were out of time. Frustrated beyond words, they went off to bed. My husband sat down in the midst of all those little plastic pieces, determined to solve the problem. Before long, he was lost in K'Nex heaven; he didn't quit until, without quite meaning to, he'd finished the whole thing. Early the next morning, Henry and Jack came running into our room, shouting, "The brownie made the whole merry-go-round! He finished it for us!"

Somehow, in our hurry to steer our children toward accomplishment and independence, we seem to have forgotten what childhood is all about. Preoccupied with managing their lives, and our own, it is so easy to lose sight of our children—their tenderness and innocence, their joyousness, their capacity for wonder, their hunger for enchantment. A touch of magic can reawaken the childlike spirit in all of us, allowing us to revisit, for a time, the secret realm of childhood. In a beautiful passage in her journal, called *Falling Through Space,* Ellen Gilchrist describes the love and security she felt as a child, thanks to her mother's ability to enter into her imaginary universe. "This is my world," she writes, "where I was formed, where I came from, who I am. This is where my sandpile was. I have spent a thousand hours alone beneath this tree making forts for the fairies to dance on in the moonlight. At night, after I was asleep, my mother would come out here and dance her fingers all over my sand forts, so that in the morning I would see the prints and believe that fairies danced at night in the sand."

So much of family life is, by necessity, given over to cleaning up, hunting for what's lost, and arguing over who is going to tackle which mess. But family life also offers us opportunities to enliven our days with play. A game can dispel a grim sense of duty and replace it with a spirit of fun. A house is enhanced by the presence of unseen spirits. Magic tickles our senses. When we began to transform cleanup time into a favor for a brownie, we found that our attitudes were transformed as well, for we were creating something special together—a climate of wonder. In our house, the brownie gets credit for much of the work we parents do after the children are asleep, and in return, our children do more of the tasks we ask of them without grumbling. They may not care much about our standards of cleanliness, but they do want to keep the brownie happy. Of course, the truth of the matter is, the brownie's benign presence brings enchantment to us all.

Note: If you want to ensure the well-fed contentment of the brownie in your house, and of your children as well, there is nothing better than this porridge.

A BROWNIE'S FAVORITE TREAT

Before you go to bed at night, combine 2 cups of McCann's steel-cut Irish oats (available at all health food stores and most supermarkets) with 2 cups of water, 1½ teaspoons sea salt, and ¼ cup powdered whey or buttermilk. Cover with plastic wrap and allow to sit overnight. In the morning, combine oat mixture with 2 more cups of water in a heavy saucepan. Bring to a boil and simmer, stirring, until thick, about 5 minutes. This is the easiest, most healthful, most delicious breakfast imaginable, but it must be tried to be believed! Serve it with an array of "toppings" and let the children create their own oatmeal sundaes: chopped walnuts, brown sugar, maple sugar, cinnamon, raisins, dried cherries, and milk. Serves four, with a bit left over for the brownie. (Alternatively, you can put all the ingredients and the full amount of water into a Crock-Pot before bed and turn it on low, and your porridge will be hot and ready to eat in the morning.)

The realm of enchantment
is open to us all,
if we are willing to step
over the threshold.

GRACE

GRACE DID NOT come easily to our dinner table. When I was growing up, the oldest family member present, usually a grandparent, would say a blessing before holiday feasts, but that was all. Most nights, my mother called us to dinner, we straggled in, took our places, and began to eat. Looking back, I see a certain matter-of-fact wisdom in my parents' approach. My mother served dinner to her family every night, year in and year out, and we were expected to be there, to eat it, and to be grateful for whatever was on our plates. Food preferences and table manners weren't an issue, for both of my parents worked hard all day, my father's fuse was short, and no one wanted to be the one to ignite it.

As my own sons approached the age where we could actually gather round a table together, the whole issue of meal-time seemed worth some thought. Among the social institutions that may not survive into the twenty-first century, the family meal must certainly be near the top of the list. Our schedules pull us away from the table and each other, and fast foods invite us to eat on the run, stopping just long enough to fuel up between one activity and the next. And, as any mother who has raced home to cook dinner for her family knows all too well, we often put out far more than we get back. Is it worth all the effort it requires to shop, make a meal, and get it on the table, only to be met by children's upturned noses, adolescents' complaints, and somebody shouting that they don't have time to eat as they head out the door? Is this ritual really worth preserving after all?

I used to ask myself this question as I mopped up spilled juice, bribed a stubborn two-year-old to eat four more bites of macaroni, tried in vain to carry on a conversation with my husband, saw my own dinner get cold as I jumped up for the twelfth time to get more milk, the salt, the ketchup . . . I had to laugh when I read a meditation by a famous monk in which he suggested that mindfulness includes setting your table and planning your mealtime so well that you would not have to leave your chair once you sat down to eat. Easy for a mystic, I suppose, but impossible for a mother.

So why *do* we bother? Perhaps it is because mealtime offers us an opportunity each day to celebrate being a family. In a world that is full of change and inconsistency and uncertainty, we each have a place that is really ours, a place at our own table, and we can come together there and nourish our bodies and our souls, as human beings have done since time began.

Not long ago, a friend who teaches at an urban kindergarten told me that when she welcomed her first class to the table for snack time, she suddenly realized that many of these children had never eaten a meal at a table with other people. They had never seen a folded napkin, heard a blessing, or observed any of the conventions we associate with mealtime. Thus she devoted the first weeks of class to teaching the children how to sit next to one another in chairs without squabbling or jumping up, how to place napkins in laps, join hands for grace, say "please" and "thank you," and eat the food set in front of them. Over time, too, she was able to introduce them to the pleasure of sitting around a table with others and sharing the events of the day. But long before these children could begin to develop the art of conversation, they had to learn how to be part of a group, how to honor the ritual of breaking bread together.

Every parent I know has experienced the family dinner table as a battleground. Emotions run high here, and adults and children alike are quick to dig in their heels—over the food and how much of it gets eaten, over table manners, seating arrangements, and every aspect of behavior, from how forks are held and how food is chewed to what kind of conversation is allowed and what is not. It is tempting to run up the white flag and retreat to a pizza in front of the TV.

Yet if we give up on the very customs that bind us, we run the risk of losing each other, both physically and emotionally. The sustenance provided by food that is offered with love and served in a peaceful atmosphere is not to be found at McDonald's or in front of the evening news. Over time, my goals for our family dinnertime have changed dramatically. After too many struggles over what was on the plate, I finally realized that dinner—at least at this stage of our lives—is not even really *about* food. It is about love, and about learning how to be together. So we abandoned most of the negotiations over what and how much the children should eat. We decided to aim for congenial mealtimes instead, to turn dinner into an event that we could each look forward to, rather than allow it to become yet one more undertaking to be executed and survived in the course of the day.

To this end, I prepare good, healthful food, and I expect my children to try a bite of everything, without discussion. Beyond that, all I ask of them is that they eat what they can and refrain from comments about the meal. The last part of that sentence is the most important! As my children interpret it, it means, "Don't bad-mouth the food." I won't cook two separate meals or cater to a child's fussy tastes—but anyone who doesn't care for what's being served is free to bring his own fruit and cheese to the table—once again, *without discussion.*

Conduct and family conversation, then, become an integral part of the meal. We learn by doing. Little wonder, then, that parents can best teach behavior by example, for, like it or not, our children watch us and follow our lead. As our children have grown, so have our expectations for them, from the amount of time we ask them to sit in their chairs to the refinement of their table manners. As long as I keep the real goal in mind—a happy, harmonious gathering—it is not hard to keep the rest in perspective. I may gently guide with a glance or a hand signal, whisper a quick reminder when necessary, take a disruptive son onto my lap or even out of the room for a moment if that seems the best way to allow the mealtime to flow on without calling undue attention to anybody's lapses. It takes self-discipline for *me* to refrain from nagging my children to eat more of this or that, but I realize that it also takes self-discipline on their part to learn to sit at the table, to feed themselves graciously, and to enter into the conversation. We do our best. I will say this, though: Once our focus shifted away from food negotiations, we were all freed to simply enjoy the experience of gathering together to share the stories of our days. The mood lifted.

*I*n the same way, through trial and error, we found a way to pause for a moment before plunging into the chatter and commotion of mealtime. My husband and I agreed that we should institute the ritual of grace at our table. Wanting it and actually doing it, though, were two different matters. For a long time, saying grace simply seemed impossible—either my husband would forget, or I would, or else one child or the other would be waging war against piety of any sort. At one point, Jack, then three, protested by putting both hands over his ears and shouting, "No grace, no grace, no grace!" With no tradition of my own to fall back on, I was unsure how to proceed—we were making it up as we went along, anyway. Certainly I found it hard to summon much gratitude myself at these moments. The fact is, saying a prayer before mealtime didn't seem natural to me, either. I felt as if I were playing a part rather than expressing a genuine feeling. No wonder my children weren't buying it!

I realized that we needed to start over again, and to begin right where we were rather than trying to impose something artificial. So I simply invited each person at the table to say what he felt grateful for at that moment. There are no rules to this ritual; you are even allowed to pass if you wish. But I can't remember a single time that any adult or child at our table has skipped an opportunity to express gratitude for *something*. On the contrary. Sometimes the lists get so long that we continue them on through dinner. My sons have been thankful for rocks, baseball games, earthworms, snow days, beloved teachers, new friends, and countless other gifts both large and small. I wish, sometimes, that I had jotted down these dinner notes over the years, for what a record it would be of our life together and the blessings that have rained down on all of us. Sometimes, when it is our turn, my husband and I catch one another's eyes across the table and give thanks for each other. Our sons are reminded, then, of the love that surrounds them, even in the midst of a hectic day or a difficult week.

A couple of years ago, Jack and Henry brought a grace from their school to our dinner table. By then, having grown comfortable with a mindful pause before dinner, it finally felt natural for us to hold hands and say a short verse together:

> *Earth who gives to us this food, sun who makes it ripe and good, dearest earth and dearest sun, we'll not forget what you have done. Blessings on our meal and each other. Amen.*

Sometimes the words are rushed a bit, but we have all come to treasure the ritual, as if the very act of saying grace has itself had a cumulative effect. It is part of who we are, part of what we do. Occasionally Henry or Jack will offer a different grace they have learned, or even a song. Special holidays usually inspire special blessings. Gratitude has taken root at our table; it has become a habit, and I am grateful for that, too. Giving thanks for what we have, we become increasingly mindful of the beauty and abundance that is all around us.

I think one reason we all feel as rushed and harried as we do is that we spend so much energy just trying to meet our children's unending demands. Dinnertime can easily become just one more obligation, as we try to accommodate everyone's requests for special foods, different drinks, favorite treats. Now, I put my energy into preparing a simple meal and serving it with love. This, in itself, is no small accomplishment. Yet when we cultivate a festive mood, our meals can become celebrations in themselves. And when we stop to give thanks for the riches that are already ours, we begin to notice more and more of them; they multiply before our very eyes. The children's focus changes then—from what they want to what they have. Suddenly we are wallowing happily in our sense of abundance: a perfect pop wheelie in the driveway, ice cream for dessert, a mystery novel waiting on the nightstand, fresh corn on the cob, ten baskets in a row, a new song mastered on the piano, a sleep-over to look forward to on Friday night . . . Joy!

Family grace, like family mealtime itself, has been threatened by the pace and complexity of modern life. How easy it is to skip it. Yet how worthwhile it is to clear a space for reverence and community. Saying grace together, we are lifted up and out of ourselves for just a moment, as the light of spiritual awareness shines upon our gathering. I think of our family table as a training ground for all of life, a place where adults and children alike can learn to put aside their differences in favor of laughter and fellowship; a place where we can each be heard and respected; a place where each of us can offer love and nourishment and receive it in turn. When we hold hands around our table, we create a sacred space there. When we share food and life and good talk, we reweave our connections with each other.

*J*f your family has lost touch with the simple pleasures of mealtime, the following suggestions may inspire you to return to the table together.

∼ Few of us can manage a family dinner every night of the week, but we can surely commit ourselves to one or two. If you can't come together at dinnertime, do Sunday breakfast instead. Be flexible with the arrangements, but honor your commitment to the goal of gathering as a family to nourish bodies and souls.

∼ Create a mood of warmth and celebration at your table. Light candles, arrange place settings with care, pick a bouquet of flowers, or invite your children to devise a centerpiece. We use candles nearly every night throughout the fall and winter and usually cloth napkins and placemats, too. Children love ceremony and, given the opportunity, will generally rise to the occasion. Even a humble meal is enhanced by candlelight and a sense of festivity.

∿ Agree that TVs and stereos and other background noise will be turned off, so that you can tune in to each other. Let the answering machine pick up the phone. If you treat your time together as a special occasion, your children will, too.

∿ Keep conversation to subjects that invite everyone's participation. This is not the time to air the day's grievances or describe the latest controversy at the office; enjoy one another's company instead. Our family has had great fun with a couple of decks of TableTalk cards, each of which asks a provocative question meant to get everyone thinking and talking. An adult and a children's version are available, and we love them both. One card is all you need to launch a theme that can engage everyone's imagination.

∿ Figure out what is most important to you at mealtime, and try to achieve that. Keep the ground rules firm and simple. For example: I require my children to try one bite of everything, to refrain from complaints about the fare, and to carry their plates to the sink when they're through. Be realistic in your expectations and relaxed about the things beyond your control. Strive for harmony. Keep the mood light, don't get sucked into arguments, and remember to aim for progress, not perfection.

∾ Excuse the children when they have finished their meals, and then treat yourself to some adult time and some adult conversation. Our children now know that their father and I expect to be left alone for a few minutes at the end of dinner, and they've learned how to keep themselves occupied while we have our time. Even when I'm home alone with the kids, I still allow those quiet moments. Just because children are capable of eating a meal in ten minutes or less doesn't mean that we have to.

∾ Be spontaneous. One dark, rainy afternoon I found myself out on the road at four o'clock, running errands with two tired, hungry children in the backseat. My husband was out of town for the night, and it suddenly occurred to me that there was no rule requiring dinner at six. We could have tea at four-thirty instead. I pulled into the bakery for scones and cake, and we headed for home. While the kids set the table with china teacups and flowered napkins, I cut cheese into little cubes,

washed strawberries, made tiny peanut-butter
sandwiches, arranged our treats on pretty plates,
and brewed a pot of mint tea. My two robust sons
were completely enchanted. We sat down together, lit the candles, and feasted until not a
crumb was left, just delighted with ourselves.
There was no need of dinner, and the rest of the
evening stretched before us like a gift.

～ Invite guests to dinner. A guest is a surefire way to
turn an ordinary meal into a celebration. Children
love to make room at the table for one or two
more, and they are as delighted to have *their*
friends over for dinner as we adults are to have
ours. When we open our doors and our arms to
others—to both children and adults—we express
our love and caring through our deeds. Nothing
makes a person feel more appreciated than to be
honored and nurtured at a loved one's table. Children of all ages adore the hustle and bustle of dinner party preparations when they are allowed to
take part, and they also learn just how much work
and planning go into a special meal. Henry once
planned and cooked an entire meal for his baby-
sitter and her boyfriend with only minimal help
from me. Last New Year's Day, Jack invited four
young friends for a dinner party of his own devis-
ing. He hand-delivered invitations the day before
(having determined that the kids in the neighbor-

hood were being left out of the New Year's Eve festivities). The children decorated leftover party hats from a neighbor's bash, blew noisemakers, and created their own personal pizzas with English muffins, cheese, and sauce. Jack considered the whole affair a great success and was proud to have been allowed to play host.

Remember that children are spiritual beings, and as such they deserve our respect and reverence. Children who grow up in an atmosphere of thoughtfulness and courtesy become thoughtful and courteous themselves. A friend told me that in her family it is customary for everyone to thank the chef. Her young son is not the most adventurous eater, but he has mastered the art of the compliment, as she discovered recently when the two of them sat down to lunch: "This hot dog is delicious. I know you didn't *make* it, but it's just the right temperature!"

It is so easy to skip the "frills" when it comes to feeding children. We're in a hurry, they could care less—so we are tempted to dump Cheerios into a plastic bowl, hand them a sandwich, and get on with the business of life. But our sons and daughters learn the hearth's powerful lessons right here, in their own homes, at their own tables. When we honor our human need for nourishment, both physical and spiritual, we teach our children respect for their bodies and for themselves. When we practice mindfulness ourselves, our children become more mindful. And so even if we are offer-

ing an after-school snack to a five-year-old, we can do so
with love and attention. We can pour milk into a favorite
glass, arrange a sliced apple on a plate, fold a napkin, and sit
down for a few minutes to share the experience, to honor
the moment, to lend an ear.

Our own family life is not exceptional by anyone's standards. Over the years there have been mealtimes that ended
in tears, there have been more rushed breakfasts than I can
count, more harsh words at the dinner table than I care to
remember. But there have been many more moments in the
midst of my ordinary, everyday life with my husband and
children that have really been exceptional. Moments in
which we were bathed in grace, moments when we were astonished by the simple joy of our togetherness, by our delight in each other's remarkable, irreplaceable presence on
this earth, under this roof, in this family. So we do hold
hands each day, and we give thanks. "Blessings on our meal
and each other."

> *At feasts, remember that you are entertaining*
> *two guests: body and soul. What you give to*
> *the body, you presently lose; what you give*
> *to the soul, you keep forever.*
>
> —EPICTETUS

Rhythm

I RENTED THE LITTLE cabin on a whim, from a classified ad in the back of an alumni magazine. What better way, I thought, to slow the tempo of family life than to spend a week on a remote lake, with only each other for company. As it turned out, my husband couldn't get away from work that week, so we agreed that the children and I would set off together on our own adventure and that he would join us for the weekend. I learned many lessons during that week on my own with two boys, but the one that I carried home most gratefully concerns our human need for rhythm—a need that often goes unmet in our fast-paced culture.

Far away from our familiar possessions and routines, surrounded by water and woods, I had to find a rhythm that would sustain us. We had to create a cabin life. Within a day, we knew where the turtle liked to sun himself at noon, and we had begun to track the activities of the blue heron who made this lake his home. We carried jugs to the rowboat and rowed across the lake to fetch clean drinking water from a spigot on the other side. We picked blueberries and blackberries from the bushes around the cabin, watched frogs, swam in the dark, deep water, and explored the perimeter of the lake by boat. But the days were long, and the only structure was the one that I imposed: three meals a day on the screened porch, a swim in the morning, a rest after lunch, a game of Clue each night by lantern light, stories before bed. The nearest store was twenty minutes away; the nearest neighbors, strangers anyway, accessible only by boat. We really were on our own—an unfamiliar feeling for all of us.

Each night I asked Henry to set the table as I prepared our dinner. He was glad to have a job to do and willingly carried plates, silverware, and napkins out to the porch. In fact, Henry had been setting our table at home for months, but there was still quite a gap between his execution of the task and my idea of a job well done. He would not bother to fold the napkins or arrange the silverware and made no attempt to place plates neatly on placemats or to create an orderly arrangement. Sometimes I would call him back and show him what I expected; other times I just let it go. Like every mother, I choose my battles, and this one never seemed worth waging.

Yet at the lake, this mundane chore was gradually transformed—without a word from me. One night the napkins were folded; on another, the silverware was separated, forks on the left, knives and spoons on the right. Finally it was Friday—Dad was here at last! As I stirred a pot of pasta on the stove, Henry began to set the table. Fifteen minutes later he called me in to see his masterpiece. A plastic glass full of wildflowers sat at the center, surrounded by stones and colored leaves, a blue-jay feather, and a curl of birch bark—the treasures we had gathered throughout the week. The napkins were folded, each piece of cutlery perfectly placed, plates and glasses neatly arranged on placemats. "I think this is the best job I've ever done setting the table," my son said simply. It was. Bit by bit he had found the rhythm. He had learned to set a table with love.

A jazz musician once said, "If you can't find your rhythm, you can't find your soul." Rudolph Steiner, founder of the Waldorf School, believed that rhythm is life. Certainly when we are living and working in harmony with others, when our days have a shape and a purpose that flows into a larger whole, when we feel rooted in a place and in touch with the natural world around us, we feel safe and secure. Children who grow up in such an atmosphere know what it is to be grounded in themselves and to feel at home in the world.

But it is a challenge for us to incorporate rhythm into our daily lives. To do so, we must commit ourselves to order and routine; to a slower, more deliberate pace; to intention rather than to happenstance. In other words, we must develop a sense of ritual. Only a few generations ago, human activity was, by necessity, informed by the rhythms of the natural world: we slept when it was dark, rose with the sun, planted and harvested according to the seasons, experienced profound connections between the cosmos and human consciousness. Modern life has severed those connections. The pace of our society has speeded up to such an extent that many of our lives are, in fact, arrhythmic—frantic, stressed, cut off from nature and from one another. Yet if we are to create rich, meaningful family lives, we must find ways to bring rhythm back into our days.

There are moments in every day that invite my reverence—but that I simply miss because I am in a hurry or because my attention is elsewhere. Rituals are pathways back to rhythm, to the universal pulse that sustains us all. There at the lake, stripped of our regular schedules and distractions, all of life seemed to invite our celebration. The setting sun inspired us to sing each night until it vanished behind a distant ridge; the full moon invited us to turn off all the lights and spin an eerie tale; having become intimate with the birds and chipmunks who shared our clearing, we felt it only natural to bring them offerings each day of nuts and berries. These were the small rituals that brought rhythm to our days, that gave shape and meaning to our week together.

Slowing down, we become attuned to the graceful arc of a day, from morning's sleepy hugs to the bedtime rituals that mark evening's close. Rhythm returns our attention—gently, yet over and over again—to the present moment, to the ebb and flow of hours, days, and seasons; to the familiar refrains of our own souls. When we begin to celebrate life moment to moment, we show our children that their own lives are also worthy of observance and celebration. Henry knew how to set a table before he spent a week at a lake, but there—with no reason to rush from one activity to the next—his own sense of ritual and ceremony grew deeper.

Of course, slowing down in a cabin on a lake takes little effort—just an openness to each day's gifts. The challenge was to carry this rhythm home and to weave it through the busy fall days ahead. Often enough, I do find myself speeding up, trying to pack too much into too little time. But children find contentment and strength not in the day's array of activities, but in consistency, and in the familiar, homely routines that give each day its shape. So I remind myself to fall back into a gentle step, to protect our routines, and to preserve our rhythm as a family.

*Y*esterday, the warm autumn sun was a benediction, for the newspaper was predicting frost. Jack ran through the yard, arms outstretched, catching falling leaves in his baseball cap. Then we spread his brilliant windfall on the kitchen counter, choosing perfect leaves to press between the pages of the telephone book and selecting others to put at each place at the dinner table. Ritual, rhythm, love.

Once we begin to see our lives within our own families as opportunities for spiritual development, the possibility of inner growth is unlimited. Home is no longer just a place to eat and sleep, but a school for our souls and spirits. Each day yields its lesson, and our children and partners become our teachers. We find our rhythm and learn to harmonize. We learn how to cherish and care for one another and how to care for our own souls as well. We learn to dance together, how to lead and when to follow. In so doing, we bring about changes both large and small, for our children, nurtured by rhythm, may ultimately heal and restore the rhythm of the world.

> *Rhythm is our bridge between*
> *spirit and matter. Crossing it, we*
> *move from preoccupation into reverence.*

TRUTH

*M*Y CHILDREN LOVE stories, but they place an equal value on truth. Just as the dragon is about to approach the castle or the princess to prick her finger, they will invariably stop me with an urgent interruption. "Mom, is this *true*?" How is a storyteller to answer?

"Well," I might say, "I heard this story myself many years ago, and I always believed it to be true." Or, more simply and to the point, "It is as true as true can be." Children want nothing so much as to believe, and they tend to place a high value on stories that are "true life." What, after all, is the point of giving yourself over to a story that your mother simply made up? Why bother?

On the other hand, there are different kinds of truths.

The classic fairy tales have endured through the ages because they embody certain truths of the soul and human spirit; the archetypes of good and evil, innocence and knowing, possess a timeless validity that children respond to on a very deep level. We may shy away from the evil jealousy in "Snow White" or the heartlessness of "Hansel and Gretel," but our children will always pull us back. They know that these stories are important and that they get at truths of human nature that are often difficult for us to confront. I read of a teacher who recalled meeting one of her former pupils, now a young woman of twenty-five. "We used to get so put out with you," the young woman said. The teacher asked her why. "Well, you used to tell us these wonderful stories," the former student responded, "and when we asked you if they were true, you said, 'We'll see.' But of course, we all knew that they were true."

*T*ruth is a tricky subject. When children ask for truth perhaps what they are really asking for is permission to believe—permission that we parents ought gladly to bestow. The material world will crowd their consciousness soon enough. In the meantime, it is our job to nourish their soulful relationship with the world and all its creatures, including those who live in other realms, such as the imagination. Let us protect our children's immeasurable capacity for faith in the extraordinary for as long as possible.

I came face-to-face with such faith when my older son

lost his first tooth. Somehow the tooth had come out and disappeared during dinner, and it wasn't until I was brushing Henry's teeth at bedtime that I realized it was gone. What a letdown! After all those days of anxious wriggling, he had nothing to leave for the tooth fairy. I suggested that she might be sympathetic to a note. "My tooth fell out today, but I can't find it," Henry dictated. "I am sorry you can't have my tooth. I will try to save the next one for you." We put the note under his pillow, and I tucked him in. Suddenly, though, as his light was about to go off, he had many questions about the tooth fairy. "How will she know that my tooth came out?" he wondered.

"That's the tooth fairy's job," I said. "She will know."

"Will she really look under my pillow?"

"Yes, she will."

Then, with the slightest tremor in his voice, he asked, "Will she touch me?"

This was harder. "Don't worry," I said with all the maternal confidence I could summon. "Just go to sleep now. The tooth fairy will come while everyone is sleeping, and tomorrow you will find a treasure under your pillow."

Silence. Then, softly, "Is it magic?"

"Yes," I whispered back without a moment's hesitation.

"I love you, Mom," my son said with all the feeling that could possibly be contained in the heart of a five-and-a-half-year-old boy.

The memory stays with me all these years later because I knew, even then, that this was one of those rare occasions when I had come up with exactly the right answer at exactly the right time. All I needed to say was "Yes." Perhaps, deep down, at some level, my son knew the "truth," but it was the idea of magic that let him go easily to sleep that night. Sometimes we try to explain too much. Or we equivocate in order not to say something that isn't absolutely true. But there is a kind of truth that doesn't have to be literal; there is an emotional truth that sometimes better serves us all.

Now Jack is coming home from kindergarten, his pockets full of rocks to be turned into gold, and sandwich crusts to leave on the hearth for the hungry brownie who creeps out each night for a secret snack. Jack offers daily progress reports on his own loose tooth, eager to make the passage into his older brother's society of gap-toothed grins and quarters under the pillow. But I am in no hurry to see him go. For now I'm content to let him renew my own sense of magic and wonder. Emptying his pockets over the washing machine at night, I am reminded of the endless possibilities he sees before him as he makes his way in the world each day, of the magic he still knows to be the truth.

When I honor my child's faith in magic,
I extend the realm of the possible.

HELPING

*T*HIS YEAR, THE first real chill of autumn swept in with six days of October rain. The season's last tomatoes fell from the vines before I could get to them, soft and waterlogged, food for the ants. The cosmos and sunflowers, summer's final offerings, were vanquished overnight, laid flat by rain and wind. The cat, who had prowled outdoors since May, slipped through my legs and made a dash for the top floor and his winter refuge among the pillows on the spare bed. All week long, the children slopped to and from school, leaving soaked boots and raincoats in heaps at the back door each afternoon and heading straight upstairs to rummage deep in closets for last year's fleecy sweatshirts and cozy pants. By Saturday we had all had enough of doing battle with the elements. Summer was truly over. It was time to bake bread.

The media tells us that cooking is drudgery. What better way to sell more fast foods and heat-and-serve dinners than to convince us to stay out of the kitchen? Or at least to get in and out of there fast! But children know better. They are drawn instinctively to the warmth of the hearth and the magic doings that go on there. If you have become a jaded cook, just hand over your wooden spoon to the nearest child and ask for help. Flipping pancakes? Need an egg cracked? They are delighted to offer their services, for they know, of course, that cooking is play. Best of all, though, it is play that results in something good to eat. Surely making food from scratch is one of childhood's simplest pleasures— and the source of a great sense of accomplishment as well. Even a child of five can feel pride in his ability to feed himself and his loved ones.

Most children are eager to help—whether in the kitchen, out in the yard, or with the mundane chores of family life. Often, I find myself tempted to rebuff my sons' eager offers of assistance just because, in most instances, it *is* easier to do a thing myself. But I miss out then on an opportunity for growth, both theirs and mine. So I try to let them try. It used to be that work was a regular part of children's lives. There were chores enough for everybody, and then some, and children were expected to pull their weight as soon as they were able. Today it is a real challenge just to find appropriate work for children to do, for our own lives have become increasingly hands-off. Still, it is worth the effort, for meaningful work of any kind builds a child's awareness of others' needs and confidence in his or her own abilities.

If we go about our own tasks with joy and mindfulness, our children grow up knowing how to take pride in their work. They will come to love the challenges life sets before them, rather than avoiding them. If we make light of the chores that must be done, children learn that work can be play. If we take up the daily work of life ourselves, rather than paying someone else to do it for us, our children learn from our efforts and will become capable adults themselves.

Work is love made visible, the old proverb says. As I sweep the kitchen floor each morning after my sons troop out the door; as I watch Jack pushing the lawn mower, his small hands between his father's large ones; as I entrust the morning's waffle making to Henry, I am reminded of the truth of those words. Here we are, working together for the good of all, enlivened by our efforts, bringing grace to our home.

My sons know that I love to cook, so they love it, too. The kitchen is the center of our family life, the place where both souls and stomachs are fed, where domesticity and spirituality are inextricably linked. Here, perhaps more than in any other room, we can find the divine in the ordinary. Children do it intuitively. They marvel at the inner workings of the pepper grinder; line up to push the buttons on the mixer; are amazed by the transformations that occur on top of the stove. As Jack often likes to remind me, "A watched pot *does* boil!" When my boys are at odds with the day, or I am, kitchen work seems to ground us all. Here, we create wonderful food to eat, and we serve it to each other. Then, working together, we restore the room to cleanliness, order, and harmony.

*B*read is particularly satisfying because it invites us—children and adults alike—to plunge in up to our elbows, to mess around on a grand scale. No two batches ever turn out exactly the same—yet the reliable alchemy of yeast, water, flour, and salt is an enduring source of wonder and fascination. If your child is old enough to dump a cup of flour into a bowl, he or she is old enough to bake bread.

What a pleasure it is, after months of summer's comings and goings, to tie on aprons, pull out the mixing bowls, and settle into the homey rituals of baking. Sometimes I wonder if I am giving my children enough exposure to the world beyond our walls—the science museum's latest exhibits, the library's desert-life slide show, the rec department's mask-making workshop. There is so much for them to do, so many offerings, so many things to learn. But then I see: Jack has lovingly sprinkled cinnamon and sugar over a flattened square of bread dough and is patting it into a miniature loaf. Henry has taken it upon himself to get out the broom and dust pan and has begun to sweep the flour off the floor. The kitchen windows are steamy from the heat of our exertions, and the bread is ready for the oven. On this day, we did not rush forth. We stayed home instead and worked and played in this one good place.

My favorite bread recipe came from my friend Peyton; an old lady gave it to her; beyond that, I cannot trace its provenance. But I can guarantee the results, for I have never seen it fail to satisfy a child's creative impulse, or an empty stomach, either. This bread dough does not need to be kneaded, but it will not suffer from such a workout if you feel so inclined. It will produce perfectly well with one rising but is happy to be punched down two or three times and to spend a night in the refrigerator before baking if need be. It is, in a word, forgiving, and therefore a perfect bread to make with children. We call it "wonder" bread, because it is always good. This recipe makes seven loaves—three to eat, three to give away to deserving friends, and one to pull apart and devour right out of the oven, steaming hot and slathered with good butter and honey.

"WONDER" BREAD

Combine in a very large bowl:

>   4 tablespoons canola oil
>   4 tablespoons honey
>   3 tablespoons salt (I prefer sea salt)

Add:

>   8 cups warm water and 2 tablespoons yeast

Stir and wait 5 minutes, until yeast is dissolved.

Stir in:

>   7 cups white flour
>   7 cups whole-wheat flour
>   2 cups rolled oats (or, if you prefer, any combination of soy flour,
>   rice flour, wheat germ, oats, or bran)

When dough is well mixed (use your hands or a wooden spoon for this), scoop half of it into another large, oiled bowl, cover both bowls with a cloth, and let dough rise until doubled, about 1½ hours. At this point you can punch the dough down, divide it into loaves, and place into seven greased pans. Or you can punch it down and let it rise in the bowls again. Just make sure you punch it down well after each rising. Allow the bread one final rise in the pans. Bake the loaves at 400 degrees for about 40 minutes, or until the bread sounds hollow when tapped, rotating the pans midway through the baking to ensure even browning.

*F*or children who are simply in the mood to get their hands into dough, or for those times when the day does not allow for bread to rise, the following pretzel recipe is most satisfying. We often make these when the children have friends over to play—the whole project is done in an hour, and then there are snacks to eat or carry home. Children love to form little lumps of this dough into letters, snakes, and all sorts of whimsical shapes.

PRETZEL SHAPES

In large bowl, dissolve 1 tablespoon yeast in ½ cup warm water.

Add:
> *1 teaspoon honey*
> *1 teaspoon salt*

Add:
> *1⅓ cup flour*

Knead dough, then divide it among two to four children and let them have their way with it. They can roll little pieces into snakes, then form them into shapes or letters. Place shapes onto cookie sheet, brush lightly with beaten egg, and sprinkle with coarse salt. Bake for 10 minutes at 425 degrees.

We learn the joy of work and the gentle art of nourishing at our own hearths, with flour on our hands.

DISCIPLINE

I WOULD NOT HAVE wanted anyone to see what occurred between my son Jack and me this morning. Now, a few hours later, he is off at school, and I am still struggling with myself, wishing I could start the day over again and do it right this time. Certainly it would be easier for me to leave such an unhappy incident out of my reflections about the soul craft of mothering. Yet I do fail. We all do. So I will include this episode along with the hallowed moments, for the truth is that our daily lives with children are made up of both—the dark times and the light. And it is when we come up against our own shortcomings, and our children's, that we seek and find real insight.

It is easy for me to talk about the golden moments of

motherhood; there are so many of them. It is easy, too, to commiserate with a friend about the quirks of children and husbands, about days that are too busy and nights that are too short—this is all familiar, comfortable territory. But rage and discipline, the struggle to maintain a sense of self, even as we practice the arts of self-sacrifice and self-control—this is treacherous terrain, difficult to navigate, hard to examine, harder still to discuss.

My husband and I agreed long ago that we would not spank our children, that we would not use violence of any kind, either to teach our children or to punish them. And we have tried to honor that promise. But that's not to say that our children never get the better of us. Just as our sons have brought forth in us the very best we have to offer, they have brought us face-to-face with parts of ourselves we would have preferred not to meet at all.

By the time Jack wandered downstairs for breakfast this morning, the rest of us had finished. But with five minutes to go before we needed to be out the door, he was in no hurry. He spread out his baseball cards on the table, practiced a few tricks on his yo-yo, complained about the shirt he had to wear to school, all the while ignoring my request that he sit down and eat his cereal. As we ran out of time, I ran out of patience. He would not sit, he would not eat. So I swept him up, placed him on his chair, took up a spoonful of oatmeal, and brought it to his mouth. At which point my son let out a shattering, no-holds-barred, top-of-his-lungs scream. Deep within me, some frayed maternal wire snapped. Without thinking, I put one hand under his chin, another on top of his head, and clapped his mouth shut. When he opened it to scream again, there was a bright spot of blood on his tongue from where he had bitten the inside of his cheek. He was outraged, hurt, eyes wide with pain and disbelief. And there it was—my own failure, as shocking to me as it was to him. Who was the one in need of discipline here after all, him or me?

The answer, I know, is me. I lost my temper and, unintentionally, I hurt my child. So as I sit here now, I am less troubled by his unacceptable behavior than by my own. I suspect there is no loneliness in the world more painful, and shame filled, than that of a woman who has just hurt her own child—unless perhaps it is the loneliness of the small child who has suffered at the hand of his mother. We can create hell in the space of a moment, and we meet the devil in ourselves.

"He has to learn that his actions have consequences," my own mother reassured me when I called her an hour later, still shaky. "Even parents get mad and lash out sometimes."

She was right, of course, but her words didn't make me feel better. The fact is, this didn't have to happen, and it probably *wouldn't* have if I hadn't been at odds with the world myself this morning. Chances are I would have quietly taken Jack in hand sooner and avoided the meltdown altogether—or at least have been better able to cope with it when it did occur—if I had been feeling centered and mindful, instead of tense and distracted. I don't excuse his conduct or my own—but I also know that it didn't come out of nowhere. I have a tight schedule today, a meeting tonight, and an interview tomorrow that I've already lost sleep over. Jack, trusty little emotional barometer that he is, was simply acting out the way I was already feeling inside. On another day, at another time, I might have led him out of his dawdling and whining before it had a chance to escalate into something more. Today we turned on each other with waves of anger that caught us both by surprise.

Two years ago I confided to one of Jack's nursery school teachers that I felt ill equipped to meet the challenges he presented me with on an almost daily basis. "My older son is so easy," I said. "He never gives us any trouble at all."

"Well," Jack's teacher replied cheerfully, "you won't learn much about yourself from Henry, but you will certainly learn a lot from Jack."

She was not altogether right, for the fact is I've learned an enormous amount from both of my children. Different lessons from two very different temperaments, all of them valuable. But it is true that Jack—forty-two pounds of spirit, vulnerability, curiosity, and sheer life force—has been my most demanding teacher, exposing all my weaknesses and requiring me to develop even greater fortitude. In his passionate, headlong rush into life, he has shown me exactly where my rope ends, where my patience runs out, where my edges fray, where my own outer limits really are. He has taught me that in order to be an effective and loving disciplinarian, I must first be able to control myself. So I am learning self-discipline right along with him. He requires of me an inner strength that I don't always possess. So I work to keep my footing, for I have learned that my own quiet self-assurance, and my unwavering faith in his goodness, has a far better effect on him than my anger ever will. He has demanded of me a level of emotional steadfastness that I don't always possess. So I have had to go in search of my own deeper resources.

If Henry, in his loyalty and gentleness, has brought forth newfound tenderness in me, then Jack, in his struggle for self-mastery, has reminded me that discipline is a two-way street and that before I can take my raging child firmly in hand, I must first lay claim to my own composure and inner strength. I don't always manage it. But I have learned that when I "lose" it—and I know it does happen to all of us at times—it is usually because I have not taken the time to slow down and pay attention to whatever is going on inside me. When I do stay connected to my own feelings—when I am fully present and conscious of what's going on beneath the surface—then I find myself possessed of all the patience, humor, intuition, love, and strength that effective discipline requires.

*D*oesn't it seem that anger gets the best of us when, for whatever reason, we feel too confused or weak to cope with a situation? Or when we're afraid, or overwhelmed, or simply exhausted? Of course, we are only human, and there are times when we all—children and adults—feel overwhelmed. The issue, then, is not whether we can mold our children to do our bidding, but whether we can learn to ride out life's ups and downs without losing our own bearings. When we discipline by example instead of by force, we send a valuable, empowering message to our children: "Do as I do."

Deep down, Jack really does want to be good, but he is also strong willed and volatile, often at the mercy of his emotions. What he most needs from me then is not an emotional hurricane of equal fury, but just the opposite—a living example of the kind of strength and clarity that will ultimately show him the way to make constructive use of his own energies. Children need clear boundaries as they learn to master socially acceptable behavior, but they also need exposure to the art of self-control. Where else will my sons learn grace under pressure, if not right here in their own home?

To me, self-discipline goes hand in hand with a healthy, balanced life—and that includes knowing how to take care of myself when the pressure builds. Deadlines and hectic schedules and cranky children are facts of life. Try as I might to keep our days from being too full, it's not always possible. Sometimes life simply demands that we all overextend ourselves, even if only for a week here or there or a day or two. These are the times when I can least afford to ignore my own inner state, for my husband and children pay the price when I do.

Thoughtful parenting requires time to think. Yet many of us don't have time in our lives for thinking. We need to make time. Even a few quiet moments alone early in the morning will enable me to lay the foundation for a day of living and loving from the heart. I meet my children then with heightened awareness, having already sorted out my own needs and priorities and achieved some sense of inner balance. Of course, the days when it seems impossible to take this meditative time are the very days when I need it the most! But I am learning—self-discipline is not an accomplishment in itself, but an ongoing, lifelong practice, one that challenges me each and every day. Fortunately I have a great incentive to keep working at it, for I remind myself that it is not what I do as a mother, but who I *am* as a human being that will make a deep and lasting impression on my children. I can bring peace to my children only when I possess it myself.

Before Jack left for school this morning, we built our bridge back to one another. On bended knee, I brought him close. "I am sorry," I said. "I lost my temper and I have hurt you, and now we both feel so sad."

"We *are* sad," he wept, "and you shouldn't have done

that. And I'm sorry, too." Our battle over, we tended to the wounds. A heartfelt apology requires self-discipline, too, and out of the morning's chaos we cleared a place for repentance and forgiveness. By the time Jack finally left for school, his face washed clean of tears, he had put the entire episode behind him. He stuck his red baseball cap on his head, lifted his lips to mine, kissed me, was off. Yet as I write these words, I still feel sorrow for my son and for myself, for I know that despite our best efforts, there will be more pain in our future together, more tears, more hard lessons for each of us. In a diary she wrote in her eighties, Florida Scott-Maxwell observed, "Love at any age takes everything you've got." It does indeed.

It is not what I do as a mother, but who I am as a human being that will make a deep and lasting impression on my children. When I discipline my children, I must also be disciplined myself.

STRETCHING

HENRY PUT ME in charge of the lights. As soon as he stepped out on stage—the area in front of the living room couch—I turned the dimmer switch all the way up and then slipped into the spotlight beside him.

Earlier in the afternoon, as we practiced our simple duets, me on the recorder and Henry on his guitar, he asked me, "Is this your first concert, Mom?"

"Yup," I answered, "my very first."

"Didn't you ever play music when you were a girl?" he pressed, incredulous.

As I remember it, my musical aspirations came to an abrupt end one day early in second grade, when an old man with wild gray hair, dressed in a white shirt and a dusty black suit, appeared in our classroom. Mr. Kertez, with his air of profound, inexplicable disappointment and an accent that startled small children into cowed attention, had come to survey the new crop of potential students. He went from desk to desk, asking each of us to stand up, in turn, and sing the scale. Those who could carry the tune of "do-re-mi" would be sent home with notes inviting them to begin violin lessons. Mr. Kertez stood at my desk, head down, nodding slowly back and forth as I imagined myself as Julie Andrews, singing with a purity and sweetness that would surely prove me worthy of the violin. "No, no, no," he murmured sadly, moving on to the next desk and to Karen Talarico, who, it turned out, could sing on key. And that was that.

How easily children are stopped in their tracks—by a teacher's criticism, another child's taunts, a parent's offhand remark, a friend's thoughtless comment. By the end of my own ninth year, I had been pegged as a bookworm who couldn't sing, draw, or throw. So I read stacks of books, kept my mouth shut in public, and stopped moving my body.

As the mother of two boys, though, I suddenly found myself forced out of my well-worn identity and back onto the learning curve. My children needed lullabies and, later, someone to play catch with. To my astonishment, I discovered that I did have songs to sing, and an acceptable pitching arm, too. A few months ago, Henry, who inherited all of my nonathleticism, decided he wanted to try Rollerblading, and he wanted me to go with him. "Mom," he said firmly, "you're almost forty years old! Of course you can do it! I'm trying it, and I'm only nine!" He had a point.

When we arrived at the Wal-Lex Roller Rink, the PA system was blasting the Village People. Music from my distant past. I clutched my son's arm and wobbled out onto the floor, worrying about osteoporosis. Slowly I inched my way around the room while Henry picked up speed and mastered the art of stopping without crashing. An hour later, though, when the DJ put on "Blue Suede Shoes," I was ready to cut loose myself. We were having a blast. Then it hit me—my son had pushed me to try something new, just as I push him every day of his life: to play the guitar, to learn to swim, to make his own phone calls, to learn Spanish and long division.

Our kids are out there on the front lines all the time, confronting new challenges as they figure out how to make their way in the world. Meanwhile we parents tend to settle into our ruts, doing what we know best: work, commute, eat dinner, go to bed, then get up and do it all over again. We keep everybody fed and clean and on schedule—and in the process, we teach our children how to become responsible adults. But how inspiring is that? And is it really the way any of us want to live, stuck in the comfort zone? The other morning, as I was urging Jack to hurry up and get his shoes on so he wouldn't be late for school, he looked up at me and asked, in all seriousness, "Mom, is it any fun being a parent?"

I have a friend who says that a child's real job is to educate the parent. Certainly my two sons are doing their best with me. And I am learning. Watching them struggle to master new skills—from shoe tying to dribbling to writing in cursive—I am inspired to push my own boundaries out a bit, to risk a little in order to reap a lot, namely the joy of learning something new. The fact is, if it weren't for my sons, I would never have put on a pair of Rollerblades on the cusp of forty; I would not have defied Mr. Kertez after all these silent years and taken up the recorder; I would not have spent last weekend reading a stack of books about electricity (Jack's questions were beyond my grasp); I would not have believed myself capable of creating an entire suit of armor out of a cardboard box and a roll of tinfoil; and I most certainly would not have become the fearless backyard goalie that I am today. I would have missed a lot!

I have found my children to be far more accepting of my athletic and musical and artistic shortcomings than my peers were thirty years ago. And when they see me kick the soccer ball into the wrong goal, or hear me muddle my way through "Oh, Susannah" for the umpteenth time, they realize that there is value in the process itself and that we can have fun without perfection. As Voltaire said, "The best is the enemy of the good." Now that I'm a grown-up, I've finally realized that I don't have to be the "best" at anything. I can sing or run or paint a picture just for the pleasure of doing it. That has been a good lesson for me and for my boys as well. We inspire each other.

So last night I performed in my very first concert—for an appreciative audience of two, my husband and my six-year-old son. "This is Mom's first time playing music for anyone," Henry explained by way of introduction, "and she's a little nervous. But I know she'll do fine."

I encourage my children to try their wings
each time I stretch my own.

NURTURING

*R*ECENTLY I WAS talking with a wise older friend who has written a weekly newspaper column about her family's life for the past eighteen years. Thinking back to her own childhood, she remarked, "It's funny, isn't it, to think that a special moment in a child's life used to be about getting a shiny red bike for a birthday, or finally receiving a longed-for doll or a beautiful book. Quiet time alone, or intimacy with a parent, or simply being together as a family wasn't special at all—those things happened all the time. Now, though, children are showered with things, and they take all of this material abundance as their due. Every kid has a bike. If a child loses a toy, or breaks something, he or she expects to get a new one. Children take their possessions for granted. But the kinds of peaceful moments that used to be a part of a family's daily life have become rare and precious."

Her words resonated immediately. My own two children want for nothing—our backyard is an obstacle course of bikes, soccer balls and basketballs and baseballs, hockey sticks, goals, swings . . . In this day of discount stores, clearance sales, and yard sales, it is relatively easy, even for parents who are not wealthy, to provide children with all of the paraphernalia of childhood. "Things" are easy to give. It is much harder, though, to give ourselves. We can't buy time at a store or pick up someone else's cast-off hour at a neighbor's garage sale.

Most of the mothers I know feel they should spend more "quality time" with their children. We also yearn to feel a deeper, perhaps even a more spiritual, connection with our friends, with nature, with the ground beneath our own two feet. At the same time, we despair of finding those extra moments in our busy days. We are two-career families, stretched to the limit. Do the hours we spend driving the carpool, shuttling to and from after-school activities, and presiding over homework count as togetherness? Does the three-mile run before work constitute a relationship with nature? Can a friendship be sustained with a weekly phone call? Our obligations and routines seem to fill all of the available time we have—for our children and for ourselves. But they do not necessarily leave us or them feeling emotionally nourished.

In her quiet, inspiring book, *The Way Back Home,* Peggy O'Mara, editor of *Mothering* magazine, points out, "All that is really important is invisible: love, God, air." Mothers who try to put families first, she suggests, are the nobility of today, because they take care of the invisible. Certainly, taking care of the invisible requires that we change our focus, shifting away from the material world we all inhabit into the realm of the spirit. For me, this adjustment is not second nature; it requires a deliberate turning away—not only from the popular culture at large, but also from the well-defined responsibilities of my daily life. It demands, instead, a willingness to answer a much fainter call, a call that is easy to ignore, or to miss altogether, given the pitch of modern family life.

When the mail lies in unopened stacks around my desk, when the laundry overflows the hamper, when a work deadline looms on the horizon just a month away, I don't even have to look at my to-do list—the to-dos are right in front of my nose. The only question is which job to tackle first. I pride myself on being a productive, well-organized person: clean sheets on the beds, clean children in them, food in the refrigerator, and money in the bank. . . . As a good Yankee girl descended from New England farm stock, I know how to make optimal use of every hour; in my family, goodness and self-worth were achieved through hard work. The earlier you get up in the morning and get to it, the better person you are. My father, in his sixties, still rises before dawn and hangs a flashlight around his neck so he can clear a little brush out in the yard before seeing his first patient of the day at seven-thirty.

Yet the to-do list that I update each morning does not

begin to reflect my feelings about what's really important. I know there is more to life than being productive and that goodness is not found at the bottom of an empty laundry basket, or in the bottom line of an annual report, or even in the last line of the book I'm finally writing. And happiness is not found there, either.

I used to feel guilty about idle moments. Time spent splayed out in the lawn chair, staring at the sky, was time "wasted." A walk in the woods with a friend and her dog meant that I wouldn't get my aerobic workout for the day. When Henry, at three, wanted to hear the same story every day for a month and have the same conversation about it every time, I could not help thinking about the stack of unread library books that was gathering dust in the meantime.

But I have come to believe that all of these activities are essential. They are what is meant by "nurturing." As the writer Julia Cameron reminds us, "So much of what we need, so much of what we want, is to be savored, cherished, cared for and cared about. So much of what is missing is tenderness." Our children do not need any more possessions to be happy; they need only to feel sure that they possess our hearts, our attention, our acceptance of who they are.

*I*n the moment my first son was delivered out of my body and into my arms, the world tilted. Miraculous life! How fiercely I loved him, and how urgently I plunged into my new vocation, this career of the heart called motherhood. At the time, I had no idea how I would nurture this tiny infant through his journey into manhood. Don't spank? Spend quality time? Build self-esteem? Buy organic food? These were the themes of the parenting books I had pored over through nine months of pregnancy. But how little I really knew, as we embarked on our new life together. And how quickly, it seemed, the days were eaten up by the details of parenthood—feeding, diapers, ear infections, housework. . . .

It took a long time for me to begin to develop anything that might be called a philosophy of mothering. Most nights, I felt it had been all I could do to get through the day. Yet slowly, by increments, I found my way. Three years later, Jack was born. With our family complete, I began to sense where I really needed to be and what I needed to be doing from one moment to the next. Surprisingly, that meant learning to loosen my grip on the work ethic I was raised on. It meant letting go of certain expectations—of myself and of my children. I needed to accept that in order to mother fully, I had to take time for myself, and that I could not meet my children's demands 100 percent of the time.

But I also discovered just what it is that they need more than anything else: me. My full attention. My face in front of their faces, making eye contact. My unfailing belief in their best selves. My joy in their existence. My nurturing.

My children are most at ease when I am at ease myself, when our days are not too busy, our activities not too ambitious. They are happy when we are simply together, moment by moment, engaged with each other. No book or toy or store-bought treat can substitute for the more precious gift of my attention. The same goes for my husband. Our lives are full, and we negotiate the details of each day's demands, but our relationship requires more than synchronized calendars and shared workloads. He, too, needs to be nurtured. So I have come to think of this loving attention as my special province. I try to devote some small part of every day to taking care of the invisible. Yesterday that meant spending an hour in the hammock with Jack, inviting the cat to join us, as we read "Punia and the King of Sharks" three times in a row. Last night it meant giving my husband a back rub by candlelight as an autumn storm whipped up outside. This morning it meant sitting down with my two boys and talking gravely about the way we speak to one another in our family and about the hurts they had inflicted on each other yesterday. Humble moments all—yet it is possible to cast them in a golden light. This is the divine work we mothers do; perhaps, for a time, it is our vocation—taking care of the invisible.

When we commit ourselves to nurturing, suddenly it seems that those fleeting moments of togetherness that we do have with our children become infused with love and meaning. We become more conscious of the mood we create when we are with them, whether we're bestowing a good-bye kiss at the door, driving them to school, eating dinner together, or tucking them into bed. All of these mundane activities can be enriched; all offer opportunities for connection. When we give our children our full attention, we are already living more thoughtfully and deliberately. You may find yourself pausing to meet your child's gaze rather than hurrying her on her way. You may begin to look forward to the intimacy of your early-morning commute to school. Meals may begin to take on an air of celebration; and evening rituals may become imbued with a special quality. Simple gestures—the motions we all go through every day—can become significant when they are carried out with love and attention.

As Mother Teresa wrote, "We must not think that our love has to be extraordinary. But we do need to love without getting tired. How does a lamp burn? Through the continuous input of small drops of oil. These drops are the small things of daily life: faithfulness, small words of kindness, a thought for others, our way of being quiet, of looking, of speaking, and of acting. They are the true drops of love that keep our lives and our relationships burning like a lively flame."

Taking care of the invisible means paying attention to my own physical and spiritual health, to the inner workings of my marriage, to the emotional security of my children, to our need for fun and play, to the quality of our relationships. I remind myself that the slow, open-ended hours I spend with my sons are not without purpose; they are, in fact, a precious gift, islands of repose in the midst of life's onrushing stream. The secret, I think, is this: When we take care of the invisible, we find ourselves cared for in return. Supported and refreshed, we find the strength and forbearance to take care of the rest, too.

When I take care of the invisible,
I find myself cared for in return.

SABBATH

WE ARRIVED READY to work. My husband had loaded the car with paintbrushes, dropcloths, and turpentine, and we'd set aside our own weekend chores in order to help a couple of exhausted friends who had been laboring day and night to turn a "handyman's special" into a home. Not surprisingly, they were weeks behind schedule, frantic to finish by winter, and grateful to anyone willing to put in a few hours with a paintbrush. But when my husband and I arrived early one October Sunday with our two boys, Lisa and Kerby met us at the door with a bag of groceries. "We've been at this all week," they said. "Let's go on a picnic."

An hour later we spread a blanket in a rocky clearing at the edge of a secluded lake. The trees were aflame with autumn color under a crisp blue sky, the summer vacationers had long since returned home, and we alone were there to luxuriate in this resplendent day, spread out before us like a buffet for the senses. The boys and dogs tramped through the woods while we adults built a fire and sat around it, talking and sipping coffee. After a rambling walk to the top of a nearby hill, we cooked hamburgers over a makeshift grill and watched the sun make its way across the sky, losing warmth as it slid behind the western pines. At some point during that long, slow afternoon, as I added another sweater and marveled at the sense of utter peace and contentment that had settled over our little group by the water, I suddenly realized what we had created—a Sabbath.

For most of us, Sundays have become just like every other day of the week—a scramble to get some work done, the errands run, the groceries bought, the homework finished for Monday morning. Until recently, the only thing special about Sunday in our household was that we would buy a box of doughnuts for breakfast and drop a ten-pound newspaper (which no one ever had the chance to read) onto the kitchen table. Sunday was a day on which to dash from here to there, trying to get some sort of a jump on the week ahead. My head told me this made a lot of sense—be productive all weekend, have an easier week as a result. But it never seemed to work that way. There's always more stuff to do than time to do it in, no matter how I spend my Sunday. What's more, my soul was begging for a break.

In years past, Sunday was often the day when hardworking families switched gears. Church services and Sunday school, pot roasts at noon with the extended family gathered round, a prayer of thanksgiving, family jokes and stories, an afternoon nap, a stroll at dusk. Those are the memories—familiar, homely, redolent with good smells and a sense of time's slow stretch—that many of us carry deep within us. My mother still recalls the guilt she felt when, as a college student, she went out to a movie on a Sunday. In her family you were not allowed to mop a floor, darn a sock, or mow grass on the Sabbath. She and her sister could read to each other, practice the piano, or play a board game (but not cards!). Anything that smacked of work or popular culture, however, was out of the question.

Of course, real life in today's world is another matter altogether. Given a day off, we fill it. We may squeeze in a few hours at our desks, dash to an aerobics class, make a run to Home Depot, another to Stop & Shop. . . . Working parents, determined to make up for a week's worth of lost time with the kids, stuff the weekend with memorable treats. But what we all need—even more than a new leaf blower, a trip to the multiplex, or even a drive to the farm stand in the country—is to stop moving. We need time for stillness, time that is devoted to the soul's own purposes.

Over the last year, we have reshaped our family's Sundays. Instead of making them simply an extension of the work week, we have allowed them to become sacred. Now, Sunday *is* special. It is the one day on which we are simply not busy, the day when to-do lists are laid aside in favor of spiritual refreshment. On a practical level, this means no errands (we do them on Saturday or let them wait); no trips to the grocery store (we won't starve); no material consumption (whatever it is, we don't really need it); and a focus on the family (this is what our two boys really want, anyway). It wasn't easy, at first, just to do this much—or, rather, this *little*. And we're still trying to figure out exactly where to draw the lines, playing it by ear even as we try to honor the spirit of our commitment to Sabbath time. I will deadhead the rosebushes or plant peas, but I won't pay bills—for I can hear Sabbath's secrets in my garden, but not at my desk. I might make a pot of soup if the spirit moves me, but I don't feel obligated to cook. Often, come dinnertime, we opt for Chinese. We don't arrange playdates for the children or social engagements for ourselves, though we are open to whatever good thing comes our way. In other words, we let the day unfold on its own.

Staying put soon became a challenge that we all embraced, for we discovered something wonderful in our newly enforced leisure—unexpected moments of grace. An unplanned day will, at some point, find its rhythm and assume its own shape. Somewhat to my surprise, Sunday has become everyone's favorite day. The mood is different, mellower, and this suits our two sons as much as it pleases my husband and me. "This is the day the Lord hath made," begins my son Henry's favorite psalm. "Let us be glad and rejoice in it." So we linger over breakfast pancakes, listening to the Brandenburg concertos. We divvy up the newspaper and pass it around. We go to church, after years of believing that we didn't have time for church. We putter in the yard or take a walk in the woods. We make music. The kids sit in my lap. I sit in my husband's lap. We laugh and get silly. We play. By Sunday night—having experienced the pure joy of doing nothing much—we feel recharged, ready to take up residence again in our day-to-day lives.

In Hebrew, the word *shabbat* means to rest. For me, Sabbath has come to represent as much a state of mind as a day of the week. It means time out for the soul, time to lay aside my daily cares in favor of spiritual refreshment. It is a way of separating time into different parts and experiencing it in different ways. I do not feel that I am losing any time by spending Sunday morning in church and Sunday afternoon with my family. On the contrary, I am taking time back.

Honoring the soul's need for Sabbath time,
I relax into the here and now. I make room
for the presence of spirit.

∫PIRIT

MY SON'S THIRD-GRADE class had been studying the Old Testament, and Henry was eager to bring these stories home to us. One night before bed, we read about Moses receiving the Ten Commandments from the Lord. Afterward, as I tucked Jack in, he said, "Mom, I've *never* heard the voice of God."

"Well," I said slowly, stalling so I could compose a reply that would make sense to him, "when you have a problem, or are worried about something, if you sit very, very still and are very quiet, and wait for an answer, it will come to you. And that is from God."

"Oh," he answered, "so it's like God just sends some thinking right down into me. Well, you know, He does that every day." Jack went to sleep content that night, feeling very close to God indeed.

Over and over again, I am reminded that most of what I know of God, I have learned from my children. From the instant they arrived on this earth, squashed and bloody and astonishingly alert, they have been my teachers, messengers sent from beyond who force me to confront my own deepest questions and beliefs. Surely in those first moments after birth, when we come face-to-face with these diminutive souls entrusted to our care, we do catch a glimpse of God. We know what it is to be blessed. Our children arrive, as Wordsworth wrote, "Not in entire forgetfulness, and not in utter nakedness, but trailing clouds of glory . . . from God, who is our home: Heaven lies about us in our infancy!" Life as we know it is suddenly transformed—by the arrival of six new pounds of humanity. Few would deny the presence of spirit then, for in giving birth, we experience a profound awakening ourselves, perhaps even a heightened consciousness. But is there a way to sustain that spiritual connection as we set about our tasks as parents? How do we nourish our children's souls as they grow and begin to challenge us? Where, in our complex lives, does spirit live and flourish?

For me, mothering itself has been a spiritual journey, a process of learning and becoming that has as much to do with my own inner development as with the growth of my children. Seeing the light in their eyes, watching them embrace the world, I realize that my real task is not to imbue my sons with faith or religious doctrine, but simply to create a safe and loving place in which their own souls can unfurl and bloom.

We adults may feel uncertain at times, searching for a sense of connection with something larger than ourselves. But children are spiritual beings by nature—joyful, inventive, full of faith and wonder. To join them, we need to rediscover what is important and meaningful in our own lives. We need to pay attention. And we need to honor and protect what they already possess—an innate spirituality and a real sense of intimacy with God.

A few nights ago, at an informal gathering at our church, a father asked our minister how he should take care of his son's spiritual life. The reverend's answer was simple: "Just take care of your own." Our children learn by imitation. And just as we try, through our own actions, to model for them the art of living, we can also model a way of spiritual seeking—of openness, of prayer, of faith and devotion. When we live in a way that is consistent with our own beliefs and ideals, we give our children a gift. We bring spirituality into the here and now. We teach them that deeds and words are expressions of the spirit, that our gestures speak for our souls.

As I recall the spiritual lessons my boys and I have learned together, I see that the most important moments have been those of attention and awareness. Awareness—both on their part and on mine—that our words and actions do matter, that we are part of something much greater, that all of creation is worthy of our care. I remember finding Jack, just months shy of three, stamping his feet on an anthill, squashing red ants by the hundreds. "What are you doing there?" I asked.

"Sending them up to heaven," was his reply.

On that day, we knelt together and watched the survivors go about their work. We might have talked a bit about not harming living creatures, but there was no lecture from me. Instead we simply watched for a while. Reverence snuck up on us.

Now, years later, my boys surprise me with their devotion for all life. It is at their insistence that I open windows for flies, carry spiders gently outdoors, and provide enough alternative food sources for the squirrels so that they do not disturb our garden. On the day when I grabbed our cat by the tail, called him a beast, and hurled him outside for peeing on our living room rug, I shrank in my sons' eyes. Although I apologized to the kids and to the cat, they still remember that incident with horror—and so, of course, do I.

It was Elizabeth Spencer who said, "Nothing is too small to be noticed, and once noticed, there is nothing that can't also be extraordinary." But it is my sons who show me the truth of these words, day by day, as they marvel at bugs and trees and clouds. Our walks are punctuated by discovery— "Look at this dandelion growing right up through a crack in the sidewalk!"—and musings about all of creation. It seems, in fact, that it is the small wonders of daily life that give rise to the bigger questions, as if the flower sprung from concrete is a bridge between spirit and matter, between our own brief moment here and the vastness through which we spin.

Jack: "I wonder why God made the world in the first place."

Henry: "He was probably lonely, all by himself out in space."

Jack: "Do you know why space is all black?"

Henry: "No."

Jack: "Because it's the world's shadow."

For children, spirituality is not delivered in a church sermon, nor is it an acquired skill, like reading and arithmetic. It is part of who they are, the core of their being and the source of their wondering about the world. *What's outside the sky? Where does the world end and heaven begin? What was here before the world? Did God choose you to be my parents? Why did Stefan's father have to die? Is God angry at poor people? Why did God make mosquitoes? What, exactly, is a soul?*

Their questions challenge and haunt me. I don't have the answers; all I can do is wonder with them, and share their awe at the mystery and majesty of life. But perhaps even that is enough. None of us will ever have all the answers, but we can learn, as Rilke suggests, to live the questions.

As parents, we can foster an atmosphere in our homes that embodies spirituality, no matter what our religious faith or orientation. We can acknowledge our children as divine beings, and we can live spiritually ourselves. Christina Baldwin writes in her book *Life's Companion: Journal Writing as a Spiritual Quest:* "Spirituality is the sacred center out of which all life comes, including Mondays and Tuesdays and rainy Saturday afternoons in all their mundane and glorious detail. . . . The spiritual journey is the soul's life commingling with ordinary life."

Living spiritually does not mean changing your beliefs. To me it means opening your life, making room for spirit in the midst of domesticity, work, and obligation. It means being mindful as we go about our daily affairs and cultivating an atmosphere of love and devotion in our families. We are the windows through which our children first see the world. Let us be conscious of the view.

- Share your enthusiasm for the world around you, for joy is infectious. "Enthusiasm" comes from the Greek word *enthousiasmos,* which means "infused with the divine spirit." If you are connected to and interested in all that goes on around you, your children will be, too. They will see God's presence everywhere.

- Be quiet together, and listen to the voice of spirit. Chatter is a habit, a way to fill up every nook and cranny of time—and children can become as accustomed to a stream of small talk as adults. But all those words just keep us from making our own, deeper observations. As an old African proverb reminds us, "No one shows a child the sky."

~ Make a virtue of reverence. I think of reverence as a mood of the soul, the beginning of all inner growth and development. But there is a tendency in our culture to encourage children to look critically at the world or to understand it on an intellectual level before they have had a chance to embrace and know it in a purely spiritual way. Wisdom begins in wonder.

~ Celebrate life. We tend to be so focused on efficiency and convenience that we forget to invite our children to share in life's messy or inconvenient pleasures: finger paints, late-night fireworks, mud puddles, the sunrise, baking a cake. The pure joy of a moment fully lived is more precious than clean hands, an hour of lost sleep, dry shoes, or a perfect dessert.

~ Attend to the details. When we pack a lunch, mop the floor, and fold towels with the same care we bring to the work we consider more "important," we open a path to the realm of spirit. Our whole relationship to truth, to a spiritual life, to the world itself, is contained in our gestures. Children learn devotion by example.

~ Cultivate in yourself the qualities you desire for your children. Raising children is a daunting responsibility for anyone trying to shape a family life outside the realm of commercialism, technology, and the media. But every time we reaffirm our own values we instill values in our children. When we mother from the soul, according to our inner wisdom, we teach our children to trust their own higher selves. When we stand by our convictions, we teach them strength. When we speak lovingly, from the heart, we teach our children how to love in return. When we recognize and honor the divine in ourselves and in others, we support our children's spirituality. When we live authentically and thoughtfully, we inspire our children to make their own decisions with care.

∿ Find a pathway into prayer. I did not grow up with a tradition of prayer; once again it was my children who led me. Casting about for a last-minute Christmas present that was not commercial, I decided to copy and frame a special good-night prayer for each of them, something that we could incorporate into our bedtime ritual. Little did I know, though, how deeply my sons would take these modest lines to heart. Now imbued with two years' worth of history and meaning, the evening prayers have become an indelible part of their childhood, enveloping each of them with a sense of security and love as they close their eyes to sleep. Sitting there in the darkness as we recite the well-known words, I am reminded of the preciousness of these simple, hallowed moments, of the beauty of my children, of our trust in one another and our faith in something greater than our human endeavors and concerns.

PRAYER FOR LITTLE CHILDREN

From my head to my feet
I am the image of God.
From my heart to my hands
I feel the breath of God.
When I speak with my mouth
I follow God's will.
When I behold God
Everywhere, in mother and father,
In all dear people,
In beast and flower,
In tree and stone,
Nothing brings fear,
But love to all
That is around me.

—RUDOLPH STEINER

BALANCE

*S*PREADING A PICNIC blanket under a pine tree at the spot my children have dubbed Pirate Rock, we listen to the click of nearby grasshoppers and the surf of traffic heading north on a distant highway, and revel in our secret hideaway. . . . Picking raspberries under a mild September sun, I stoop to kiss my son's berry-stained mouth, and, in a rush, tasting his salty sweat mixed with sweet raspberries, I drink in the rich abundance of this fall day, this field, this extravagant harvest. . . . I am making dinner in the kitchen, slicing tomatoes from the garden, when I am stopped in my tracks—knife poised in midair, breath caught in my throat—by the strains of "Scarborough Fair"; my husband and son are playing a duet on their guitars, and for the first time, it is perfect, and I marvel at my son's clear soprano as he reaches up for, finds, and holds his high note. . . . Rubbing sesame oil on my children as they step, scrubbed and glistening, from their bath, I am awestruck by the purity of their shining faces, the perfection of young arms and legs, the ease they feel in their own bodies. And then another day ends, and I am turning down beds, smoothing sheets, choosing the bedtime story that will meet the evening's mood. . . . Lest I ever lose perspective on what's important, may the small details of daily life serve to remind me: The sweetest memories are right here, in the moments we create and share with one another.

Yet our lives are often too crowded even to allow for such reflections. My neighbor wonders if perhaps she has overscheduled her four-year-old—and then, in the next breath, worries that if he doesn't participate in the Rookie Racquets tennis program, he will "never catch up." A friend who works part-time devotes her "days off" to running the parent-teacher association at her daughter's school and admits that her volunteer work basically amounts to another part-time job that eats up her days, evenings, and weekends. Another friend, the mother of three, spends every weekday afternoon in the car as she chauffeurs between her nine-year-old's soccer practices and Hebrew lessons, her twelve-year-old's ballet and flute lessons, and her five-year-old's playdates and gymnastics classes. Last Christmas a friend's eyes brimmed with tears as she contemplated a weekend that included three holiday parties, the arrival of her in-laws, Christmas shopping and a lunch date at the mall with a friend, her daughter's performance as an angel in a church pageant, and, if time allowed, a photo op with Santa.

Is this what we mean today by family life? Is it really the way any of us want to live? I think not. Why, then, *do* we try to do so much? Why, as one friend put it ruefully, are we "dervishing through life"? And why do we allow our children to fall victim to the same kind of overscheduling that keeps us from enjoying our own lives? I am convinced that one reason we try to do so much is because we are afraid.

What if my son falls behind his tennis-playing peers? How can I show the world I am a good mother if I don't volunteer at school? What will people think if I don't appear at that party? What will we be missing if we stay home? There is fear behind all this frenzy, fear that we, or our children, will somehow fail to measure up. But just whose expectations are we trying so hard to meet?

These days I find myself pondering another question: What do I lose when I try to do too much? The answer is simple: Balance. For me there is nothing worse than the feeling that a day has flown by without any moments of real connection between me and my husband, me and my children, me and my own inner self. Yet how easily that happens. We want so much to *do* for our children, to give them every opportunity to learn and grow and succeed. At the same time, we want to live our own lives fully, to be productive and creative and useful. Sometimes, though, we lose touch with our need to feed our inner lives and with our need for solitude, silence, and intimate time together.

*S*urely there is no one raising children today who has not paused at times to wonder: In our efforts to provide for our children, are we losing sight of what is really most important? Have our activities crowded out the kind of simple, spontaneous moments that truly make life worth living? Each and every child I know could use more of these. We adults need them, too.

A few months ago my neighbor slipped and broke her arm at work. When I called later that day to commiserate, she was joyful. "I'll have at least eight weeks off!" she said. "I can't drive, so I'll have to walk everywhere, and spring is coming. This will be great!" She was right, of course. It *was* great; life slowed down. The Saturday before she returned to her job as a pastry chef, her eight-year-old son said wistfully, "Couldn't you break your other arm, Mom?"

How easy it is to race through our lives, and to race our children through their own childhoods in the process. How many times each day do we urge our children to "hurry"? In our attempts to make the most of every day, we herd them along from one thing to the next, praising their accomplishments and urging them on to new ones. The pressure to begin mastering skills at an ever earlier age has become enormous. Even the four-year-olds I know are a busy group, their days filled with dance classes, swimming lessons, tennis for tots, T-ball, and soccer—not to mention preschool! Older children may recognize the stress of all this activity, but they know no other way to live. As an eleven-year-old neighbor put it, explaining her own conflicts among homework, music, swim team, and play practice: "Well, my whole family is crazy. We're never home. We always joke about it, but we all still keep signing up for everything."

In our town, little boys can begin their organized baseball career at four with T-ball. By seven they are playing on teams. At nine they can wear a uniform and travel by bus to "away" games. Our son Jack, watching older friends, wants that uniform already, not to mention the chewing gum and all the attitude that goes with it. It is hard for his dad and me to say no. A friend's six-year-old daughter often finds herself with two or three birthday party invitations for any given Saturday. It is hard for her mother to say no. The fact is, it requires a great deal of inner conviction to say no, both for ourselves and for our children, for we live in a society in which people are defined largely by their activities and their accomplishments. Yet if we don't set these limits, who will? If we don't say no, we become the weary victims of our own schedules. In our rush to do everything, we miss the genuine pleasure of experiencing one thing fully. When we race through life, we miss it.

*A*s mothers, we are the emotional centers of our homes. Our partners may make their own invaluable contributions, but women are still largely responsible for setting the tone and pace of family life. One of my greatest challenges each day is to sustain an atmosphere in our home that nourishes not only our bodies and intellects, but our inner lives as well. To do so, I need to have some kind of vision of where the ideal really lies. I need a sense of balance. So I ask myself, How do I want to be in the world? How shall my children spend their days? How will I spend my own? I've learned that when I'm uncertain myself of what we really need or want, I tend to charge ahead, swept up in the busyness of life. But when I take the time to examine our choices—when I make decisions thoughtfully and from the heart—I almost always end up paring down and cutting back, doing less and enjoying it more.

This quest for balance is not unique to me, or even unique to women of our generation. It has been at the center of women's lives for nearly half a century now. Indeed, finding that balance, learning how to live both fully and well, seems to me to be part of the spiritual work of motherhood. It does not come easily to any of us, and never without some kind of inner struggle.

In 1955 Anne Morrow Lindbergh left her husband and five children behind while she embarked on a solitary writing sojourn at the beach. Alone for two weeks in a simple island cottage, she found the space and quiet time to write her classic, *Gift from the Sea*. She went away, she said, in search of answers to the question of "how to remain whole in the midst of the distractions of life; how to remain balanced, no matter what centrifugal forces tend to pull one off center."

Set free from her daily obligations, and deliberately practicing the "art of shedding," she did acquire a newfound perspective on her life at home, noting, "There is so little empty space. The space is scribbled on, the time has been filled. There are so few empty pages in my engagement pad, or empty hours in the day, or empty rooms in my life in which to stand alone and find myself. Too many activities, and people, and things. Too many worthy activities, valuable things, and interesting people. For it is not merely the trivial which clutters our lives but the important as well. We can have a surfeit of treasures."

Like so many women before me, I have lived the truth of all these words. In seeking to "evolve another rhythm with more creative pauses in it," Anne Morrow Lindbergh gave voice to my own desire to live more thoughtfully and deliberately. Nursing my firstborn, wondering how the disparate pieces of my new life would ever coalesce into a coherent whole, I drank her book down in one long, grateful gulp. I cherish it still and have returned to it over and over again through the years, as to a trusted friend.

Much as I admire the clarity and wisdom of Anne Morrow Lindbergh's voice, I am equally in awe of her circumstances. Imagine: a mother of five who manages to take two weeks alone on an island, to muse and wander, to collect shells and write luminously about her search for outward simplicity, inner integrity, and fuller relationships with loved ones. The luxury of such an interlude has always seemed as extraordinary to me as the words that emerged from it. I suppose I think of *Gift from the Sea* as a kind of mother's fairy tale—a fantasy of peace and quiet that I could only dream of.

Right now, I sit at my desk with a worn copy of Anne Morrow Lindbergh's book at my side. The sun has come out after two days of rain, and the faint scent of woodsmoke drifts through my window on the damp breeze. A housefly buzzes against the window screen in a fury, trying to get out. I am tempted, as I set him free, to give in to the seduction of this fall day and follow him outside. But no, this is my time—my only time today—to write. I am ignoring the phone and postponing my other business; I have an hour and a half before I am due to pick up my children at school, and I wish only to keep my inner focus for a while longer. Soon it will be time to switch gears.

*O*ver a year ago, when I began to set these thoughts down on paper, my husband offered me a few days away from home so that I could make a real beginning, with no distractions. But life intervened, as life always does: a business trip that had to be rescheduled; a guitar recital that wasn't on the calendar; a fund-raising event that we had promised to help organize; a five-year-old's passing crisis. The weeks slipped by, and the day never did come when I could kiss my children good-bye and disappear for a while.

So I have sought to find a balance right here at home, between my regular work and this writing that I love, between my family and my other obligations, between contemplation and activity. It did not take long for me to realize that if these meditations were to reflect life as any of us really live it, then I would have to find a way to put them down right here, in the midst of life itself—in a snatched afternoon hour before three o'clock, in the quiet evenings when I find myself with some small reserve of energy to spare, in the lawn chair while my sons kick the soccer ball back and forth or flop down nearby with their own books and projects. These pages, then, do not come from a "bare sea shell of a cottage," much as I wish to know how such ease might feel. No, they come from the spare room upstairs and from the front lines of my family's life; from the ups and downs of our days together; and from my own struggle to maintain a sense of balance.

This year, we realized our family schedule would have to change. I did not want simply to add more hours at my desk, and child care for our sons. So my husband and I determined to draw new boundaries around our time. We decided that this would be *his* year to volunteer at our sons' school and that I would step back. We decided to continue Henry's music lessons, but to keep Jack out of sports and extracurricular activities at least until first grade. (At the same time, my husband promised to keep the balls flying in our own backyard—a pledge he has honored with such enthusiasm that the neighborhood kids now knock on our door and ask, "Can Steve and Henry and Jack come out to play?") We quit the health club that's twenty-five minutes from our house and joined a gym up the street instead. In fact, we made all sorts of small adjustments to our lives so that I could take on more work for a year without giving up the time we have for one another.

At first our decision to limit the boys' activities along with our own was met with protests and pleas—but these were soon replaced with a genuine sense of relief. Many days, our afternoons are free. Saturdays are our own. When Henry asks on Saturday morning, "Is there anything we *have* to do today?" I am happy to tell him that there isn't a thing. Children experience a great sense of freedom when boundaries are clearly established by their parents. My children know that I must get my work done, but they also know that I value our time together. In choosing to eliminate some of our family's activities this year, my husband and I carved out a bit more time for our kids to enjoy some of the simpler pleasures of childhood. In doing so, we managed to break away from the automatic responses—such as enrolling the boys in the same activities that their buddies were doing— and to take some of the pressure off all of us. Not surprisingly, our children seem happier and more relaxed. They enjoy the activities they do participate in, and our routines sustain us rather than exhaust us. We spend less time racing from one place to another and more time playing. Yesterday Jack and a friend took shovels into the backyard and set out to dig to China. Listening to their vivid fantasy of life at the bottom of the hole, I was grateful for the gentle contours of his life. There will be years and years for baseball, but you can only dig your way to China when you're five.

*E*ach of us has a list to make. Think about your own days and weeks. Take a good hard look at your schedule. Then do the same for your children. If they are older, ask *them* how they feel about the ways they spend their time.

    ∾ What are the things that you absolutely have to do? Write them down. If the list seems overwhelming, brainstorm some ways to shorten it. What can you delegate? Can you possibly hire someone to help? What could you eliminate if you had to? (Forget about what people will think of you if you do!) What do you want to rethink for the future? Remember, your children need you every day, and it is up to you to be in good shape for the job. You're not the only one who pays a price when you take on too much; they do, too.

~ What are the things you most love to do? Are you doing them? If not, make at least one of them a top priority. Balance means taking care of yourself as well as those who are dependent on you for their well-being.

~ What are the activities and obligations that steal your time? How could you get some of that time back? Three years ago, spurred on by a magazine article, my next-door neighbors and I formed a cooking co-op. One night a week, I make dinner for two other families as well as my own. In return, they each make dinner for our three families on the following nights. We keep the food simple and good; and those who are receiving dinner are responsible for picking it up, in their own bowls, at six. This arrangement has been a great success because it gives all of us a bit more time. If you're cooking anyway, it's easy enough to make more—especially when the payoff is two nights off.

~ Which of your undertakings get in the way of the simpler life you wish to lead? Which activities complicate your life; which truly enhance it? My friend's son hated his piano lessons and was making slow progress. She hated the hour-long commute there and back every week. But when I asked her why she was insisting on something they both dreaded, she replied, "It just seems as though he *should* learn piano. Shouldn't every kid play an instrument?" This spring they quit. Mother and son decided that they would spend Monday afternoons Rollerblading together instead—a happy decision for both of them.

So often we do things because we think we should, or for fear of being judged or left out if we don't, or because everyone else is doing them, or because our children want to sample every new activity they hear their friends talking about. But how good it feels to release ourselves from "shoulds" and to tune in to a different rhythm. To do things just for the fun of it. To have a life that is rich but not rushed, happy but not hectic.

I know now that balance is not an achievement in itself, but a journey—and I am always on my way there, never fully arrived. The world summons me countless times each day. The phone rings, the flyer arrives in the mail, the invitation is extended, the request is put forth. And I must summon the strength and clarity to know when to say "no" with grace, when to say "yes" with pleasure and conviction. I remind myself that I am not shirking my social obligations; I am protecting our family life.

"With our pitchers we attempt sometimes to water a

field, not a garden," Anne Morrow Lindbergh wrote. How easy it is to find ourselves sprinkling droplets over a field, spreading ourselves too thin, giving without replenishing, accomplishing nothing of real value. And so I strive to keep my garden small, but to care for it joyfully and well. We bloom here.

When I keep my balance, I feel empowered, for
I am guided then not by fear or pressure, but by the
small quiet voice within that whispers, "Enough."

CHOICES

THE LETTER CAME from a woman I have never met. I had just begun to write this book and was eager for my husband to have a look at the first few pieces. As he headed out the door to catch a plane to San Francisco, I pressed an envelope into his hand. That night he found himself in Palo Alto, seated next to the wife of a new colleague, comparing notes on life, kids, work—cocktail party chat. Debra told him that she had given up her career to stay home with her two children, and he mentioned the pages he had just read on his way to the West Coast. She asked if she could take them home and read them herself. When my husband hesitated, explaining that they were just a first draft and that he had another plane to catch first thing in the morning, she promised to have the envelope back to him before breakfast. So my first reader was a total stranger. Debra returned the pages with a note to me that began, "The idea of slowing down our busy lives is on my mind all the time, and it's a big topic among the mothers around here."

She wrote about her own experience as a mother and the choices she has made. I treasured that spontaneous offering, for what better way for us mothers to support one another than to share our own stories, to offer road maps of the paths we have taken? As Louise Erdrich wrote in her memoir, *The Blue Jay's Dance: A Birth Year,* "Mothering is a subtle art whose rhythm we collect and learn, as much from one another as from instinct. Taking shape, we shape each other, with subtle pressures and sudden knocks. The challenges shape us, approvals refine, the wear and tear of small abrasions transform, until we're slowly made up of one another and yet wholly ourselves." In this spirit, I share Debra's letter:

> *I am a mother of two children, ages five and nine. I had worked part time since my first child was four months old, and by the time my second child was four, I had reached my limit in juggling our crazy life. I knew it was time to stop when one day, I was driving my car and watched a mother cross the street in front of me with a shopping cart and four young children in tow. She was obviously poor and staying home with her children. I found myself envying her. She had time, and no money. I had money, but no time. Mine was a different kind of poverty.*

It seemed there was no end to the pressures we faced—school, my work, my husband's work, social events, etc., etc. Something had to change. So I just put on the brakes, held up a big STOP sign, and took a three-month unpaid leave of absence from my job. During the months leading up to my leave, I fretted and felt guilty about taking the time off. I felt it would be decadent, since my children would be in school during the day. What would I do? How would I spend my time? What would I learn?

During that leave of absence, I discovered how to just be. How to slow down, be simple, and be present in the moments of each day. And how abundant they are! I didn't hurry my children along in the morning since I didn't have to be anywhere. We could take it at their pace. Since it took my daughter fifteen minutes to get out of the car and dawdle her way into school, we left a half hour early so she could do that. We stared at trees a lot and saw nests. Oh, the list goes on. It was the nicest, slowest pace I have ever lived my life.

Things have really changed since that time. I went back to work for a few more months, then left the company. I now contract back to the same company for ten hours a week, and the flexibility allows me to keep our life on its simpler path.

I know there are lots of mothers out there who want to simplify but don't think they can. There are some female engineers at my office who say to me, "I envy what you are doing, taking this time off to be with your children. I could never do that. I feel so trapped." And I can't do anything *more than just encourage them. Really, they have to be the ones to internalize a feeling that they CAN change their reality. And then there's the other end of the spectrum. After I became a part-time engineer successfully, our group was so flexible and committed to family balance that a male engineer worked out a flexible work-at-home arrangement so that he and his wife could share child care of their infant daughter. The team was supportive, and we changed our meeting times to accommodate his schedule.*

Reading this letter, I felt as if a friendly hand had been extended across time and space. How well most of us know these longings and dilemmas! And how grateful we are when someone else recognizes and honors the small tasks we perform each day. Whenever I find myself in conversation with other mothers, we always ask one another the same question: "What's your schedule?" We want to know how other women manage, what they fight to protect, what they've decided to let go, where they draw the lines. The stories we hear may not tell us how to rearrange our own lives, how to raise our own children, how to find fulfillment. But they remind us that we do each have choices. And they may even inspire us to examine the choices we have made. Ultimately, we each have to decide where the balance lies—between work and family, between doing and being, between acquiring more and accepting what we have, between simplifying and taking on, between the world beyond our walls and the lives that we create within them. And, at some point, we may begin to ask ourselves: Just whose standards am I living by, anyway? An advertiser's? A neighbor's? A parent's? A corporation's? A culture's? Only when we stop long enough to figure out what we really care about, and begin to make our choices accordingly, can we create lives that are authentic expressions of our inner selves.

For those of us who came of age over the last two decades, such questioning may mean rejecting some of the very values that are most accepted in our culture—professional achievement over inner experience, for example, and power over moral strength. It may also mean shaping a new, imaginative picture of family life. In my own case, this picture evolved slowly, over time, for I realized when my first son was born that nothing in my young adulthood had prepared me for the opportunities and challenges of motherhood.

When I was a student at Smith College in the 1970s, the theme of my education was how we women would make our mark in the workplace. Although most of my friends and I assumed that we would eventually marry and bear children, I cannot remember a single conversation from those days in which we discussed the role children might play in our lives, or even how we might balance the responsibilities of motherhood with our careers. I suppose that if we thought about it at all, we imagined family life as some kind of adjunct to real life—that is, the lives we would create for ourselves through our careers, travels, continued education, and other worldly adventures. Our role models were out on the front lines, in business, science, and the arts—not at home with the kids. When Jane Pauley visited our campus, we packed the room to hear her speak about her first year on the *Today* show. Another successful graduate, then the editor of a top women's magazine, counseled us about the high-stakes world of publishing. There were lectures nearly every week, and they were all by women who were making it in a man's world. Jill Kerr Conway, our college president, was living proof of what was possible. Although we counted Sylvia Plath and Anne Morrow Lindbergh among our alums, we were proudest of Gloria Steinem and Betty Friedan.

It seems a lifetime ago. How little we knew, at twenty, of the real choices that would come to define our lives, or of the deeper questions that would begin to haunt us as we brought our own children into the world. My class-mates did indeed scatter into the workplace. But within ten years, most of us had also married and begun families. And although the generation just before us had left home in droves, desperate to escape the confines of parenthood, many of my peers found themselves hesitating at the door. Those who did leave were soon pulled in ways they had never anticipated. We bought and furnished our houses—and then, it seemed, no one was ever home. We had children—and then felt guilty for sending them to day care. We achieved varying degrees of material success—yet felt increasingly impoverished as our outer lives drifted further away from our inner ideals.

In time, we each came up against the same sort of questions. What do I believe in? Where do I find my sense of purpose? And then, How can I design my life to reflect that truth? What choices do I have?

I remember the first years after my older son was born as a time of isolation. The women I knew who had children had all returned promptly to work; my urban, professional neighborhood was mostly deserted during the day. My friends were happy to share their experiences of nannies and au pairs, day care facilities and preschools—but if another world of mothers and children existed, I did not hear of it. Yet my instincts were telling me that I should be with my son, that there was no real substitute for the kind of nurturing I aspired to provide. I certainly didn't feel very competent in this new role, but my husband and I both felt that we had embarked on an odyssey together, and we shared a vision of home as a safe haven in which both we and our children would grow and flourish. We talked endlessly about how we might create such a place, and as we felt our way along, we held that picture in our minds, refining it bit by bit, stroke by stroke.

In time, I did meet mothers who had made many different kinds of choices—to work part-time or not at all for a while, to create home-based businesses, to create schedules that put the needs of the children first, to share child care more equitably with spouses. The family situations were all different, the economics often presented grave challenges, yet the commitment to nurturing shone through. In time, too, I found my own rhythm and a way to combine ongoing part-time work with raising children.

More and more, though, I felt that motherhood itself was becoming my real vocation. It seemed that the more consciousness I was willing to bring to it, the more meaningful this role became. Shaping and protecting our family space, celebrating birthdays and holidays, setting a mood around the dinner table, cultivating an atmosphere in our home, painting and baking and storytelling with my sons, simply attending to the details of our lives together—these and countless other activities both large and small came to represent opportunities for deeper attention, work, and growth. Over and over I found myself both humbled and challenged by the magnitude of my task as a mother in contemporary society. Could I find a way to bring beauty and meaning to an empty afternoon, while the rest of the world spun on at a different pace? Could I confront a room full of scattered toys and see there an opportunity to transform chaos into order? Did I possess the self-discipline I needed to effectively discipline two boys? Did I have the inner strength to resist the values of corporate, materialistic America—and to shape a different set of traditions and ideals? Could I summon enough humor, patience, flexibility, and love to meet their needs from one day to the next? Was I conscious enough of my own needs to articulate them, and meet them, too? Could I let one identity fall away and begin to forge a new one out of such reflections, lessons, and feminine energies?

J think it is all too easy for us to forget, in the face of our material orientation, that most of us *can* make choices about our lives. We have the freedom—more so, perhaps, than any previous generation—to define our lives, to live according to our values, to set our own boundaries. Yet we have all been influenced, to some extent, by the pressures of our times: pressure to hire child care and return to work outside the home, pressure to foster ever earlier independence and competence in our children, pressure to own more things, engage in more activities, produce more, and buy more.

Just in the last couple of years, technology has altered the very rhythm of daily life in our culture. Our cell phones, audiotapes, PalmPilots, e-mail accounts, and laptops invite us to give up "down" time altogether. One reason we do so much is simply that we can. We may be so caught up in a cycle of bills and acquisitions, activities and exhaustion, accomplishment and recognition, that we don't even realize we have become the unwitting victims of our own ambitions and desires. But even this, at bottom, represents a choice. And it is not too late to change our minds.

Today, it seems to me, many women *are* seeking a different path. Over the last decade, women, and mothers in particular, have led the way in the simplicity movement. Those of us who came of age in a culture that undervalues the role of nurturer have realized that our families still need to be cared for. Those of us who were groomed for success have learned, from hard-won experience, that living life to the fullest does not always mean having and doing as much as possible. Those of us who have experienced corporate life have wondered whether we really want our children to follow in our footsteps. Should we be grooming them to compete in a global marketplace, or encouraging them to march at their own pace? Should we surround them with material goods, or teach them to seek and savor small, authentic joys? We may not have the answers to our questions, yet many of us are ready for something different—for ourselves and for our children.

We may have downshifted our careers or found ways to make a more equitable division between work life and family life. We may have decided to make do with less money in order to have more time. We may have experimented with new roles within the family. Or we may have begun to regard our roles as mothers in a new light—as a profound journey in its own right and a catalyst for inner growth. In any case, our focus has shifted. We have been pulled back to our own hearths, our own families, our own inner lives.

As mothers, we have opportunities each day to cultivate qualities in ourselves and in our children that are all too often neglected in our society: qualities of feeling and imagination, gentleness and compassion, reverence and wonder. As writer

Jonathan Kozol has said, "We must invest in their compassionate hearts as well as in their competitive spirits." When we bring these qualities to the world, we make our own small contributions to humankind, and to the good of all.

When I think now of my own friends and neighbors, I do so with a deep sense of gratitude for the community of caring we have formed together. We share food, chores, child care, advice, laughter, and tears—even clothes—on a regular basis. Above all, though, we share compassion for one another's struggles. Time and again we all fall short of our ideals. Life gets the best of us, or our children do. Yet we are mothers, so we go forward, loving our children and doing the best we can, from one moment to the next.

A book of inspiration discovered and passed on, an article ripped from a magazine, a phone call at the end of a long day, a walk or a cup of tea, a note of encouragement—these are the gestures by which we mothers can all reach out to one another and celebrate our journeys. We can learn to trust our maternal selves and to have faith in the innate goodness and purity of our children—even when we feel overwhelmed and the kids are pushing all our buttons. We can support one another's choices, whatever they may be. We can be understanding of each other and easier on ourselves. And we can remind ourselves that we do not need to judge our daily lives by how much we accomplish. There is real value in simply being present, for our children. For when we reclaim the realm of motherhood, we also protect and honor the province of childhood.

FOR THE CHILDREN

The rising hills, the slopes,
of statistics
lie before us.
The steep climb
of everything, going up,
up, as we all
go down.

In the next century
or the one beyond that,
they say,
are valleys, pastures,
we can meet there in peace
if we make it.

To climb these coming crests
one word to you, to
you and your children:

stay together
learn the flowers
go light.

—GARY SNYDER

WINGBEATS

IT HAS TAKEN me a year and a half to write these reflections about motherhood. Yet as I read through them now, they seem like such a modest output. So much living, after all, has gone on under this roof—and what do I really have to show for it? This handful of pages, a few moments of captured grace. I wonder why it took so long.

In the life of children, a year and a half is a very long time indeed. To me, though, it seems it was just yesterday that I sat down to compose the letter that eventually grew into this book. Yet our family life is already so very different from what it was then; even in this short space of time the details have changed, and, almost imperceptibly, we have changed with them. Only now, as I pause to look back over these pages, and over the life chapters that they represent, do I suddenly realize how much that I cherished has slipped away even as I tried to give it voice, only to be replaced by new ways of doing and of being.

My boys no longer share a tub, not ever. Now Henry showers alone, and Jack washes his own hair. And so the door has swung shut on the fantasy world they created in the bathtub, and on the long hours they splashed and played there together, emerging at last with pruney fingers and toes, to be wrapped in towels and bundled off to warm beds. Our morning cuddles are rare now, too. Jack is sleeping later, and Henry likes to be the first one dressed and downstairs. He puts on his own music, sets the table for breakfast, and basks in his newfound sense of independence. So my husband and I find ourselves alone again, arms wrapped around each other instead of around children. Both boys head off to play outside alone these days, full of their own plans and no longer in need of adult supervision or interference. Henry jumps on his bike and rides around the block; Jack walks to the pool with an older friend.

And so my role is changing, too; I am called to be less of a playmate now and more and more simply a witness to my children's own breathtaking processes of growth and inner awakening. It is with some pang of sadness that I acknowledge our endings. My days of cradling a small, soapy head in my hands; of rocking a son to sleep; of carrying a tired boy on my back; of reading "The Little Fur Family"; and of wiping bottoms and talking with teddy bears are over. And I miss them already, miss being needed that much, miss the confidence of knowing so surely where I should be and what I should be doing from one moment to the next.

Just when I figure out how to mother a kindergartner, it seems, I have a first-grader standing before me instead. I have just learned how to love and live with a nine-year-old when the nine-year-old vanishes, leaving a preadolescent in his place. They don't stay still long enough for me to have my fill of them ever, at any stage. "Stop!" I want to shout. "Let's just do it this way for a while, let's stay right here." But the movement is inexorable—up and out, away, into the future. I remember how I felt driving to the hospital to give birth to my first son, wishing even between the pangs of early labor that we could just continue on the way we were for a while more. I had gotten good at being pregnant, had learned how to care for a baby in the womb, was not at all sure I was ready to have one in my arms. Little did I know that the yearning to seize life in a freeze-frame would never really go away, or that my desire to hold on to whatever we had and whatever we were at any given moment would always be in conflict with my sons' own natural instincts: to grow up, to live, to fulfill their own destinies on this earth. Sometimes, it seems, there are discernible changes overnight. The boy who meets my gaze at the breakfast table is not the same one whose cheek I kissed the night before. And even as I marvel at the latest incarnation, I grieve for yesterday's child, already a memory. To love them is always to let them go, bit by bit, day after day.

A couple of years ago, as I sat in a lawn chair in the sun reading Thomas Moore's extraordinary book *Care of the Soul,*

I came upon a phrase that brought me to a complete halt. Family, he wrote, is "the nest in which the soul is born, nurtured, and released into life." With those few, simple words I suddenly had the beginnings of a vision of all that I aspired to in my own life as a wife and mother. If I could create such a nest—a safe haven for us all, a light-filled, sacred place in which we might celebrate life's small, authentic joys—that, I knew, would be accomplishment enough.

We live in an age in which personal experience threatens to become interchangeable, with one day blurring into the next as we eat out at chain restaurants, shop at chain stores, drive back and forth to work, abandon our souls to television, technology, and manufactured entertainment. Thomas Moore's words held out an invitation to me to go in search of something more, for myself and my family: a richer menu of sensory experiences, a more deliberate shape to our days, a more conscious appreciation for the moment at hand, and a deeper respect for the inner life. I began to realize that if I really paid attention to the quality of our days together, I could live them with more faith and joy, and fewer regrets for what might have been. If I took the time to notice things along the way, to really settle into my own life without always rushing ahead, it might be easier to weather the inevitable changes and challenges that came my way. And if we could find our own rhythm as a family, and follow it, we might all discover just what it is that is essential and meaningful in our lives.

Each spring I watch the small brown wrens in our backyard flitting back and forth with wisps of hay and leaves and bits of string as they tirelessly prepare nests for their own young. Then, eavesdropping, I hear just how demanding those new babies are, always hungry, peeping for more, more, more. But the mama birds are blessed with animal wisdom; they know that none of this will last for long, that they can do what needs to be done. Instinct guides them through the rigors of parenthood. So, too, does instinct guide us human mothers, when we stop long enough to pay attention. Motherhood offers us the chance to re-create the world anew each day, to meet it freshly, even as we discover reserves of strength and wisdom we didn't know we had. And then it is hot summer, and the nest on our back porch is empty. So soon! it seems to me. About time! thinks mother wren.

In our own nest, I hear the wingbeats every day. I count off the years in my head until my boys will leave home, and I marvel at how far we have already come from those first days and weeks together, when it seemed that infancy would last forever. Each night before I go to sleep, I make my rounds, lingering as I gaze down upon those sleeping faces, wondering where their souls are while their bodies are at rest, and where their future flights will lead them. For now, though, we are here together, safe within this family we have made, bound by our joys and sorrows and our faith in one another. If my sons learn compassion here, they will bring compassion into the world. If they learn here how to trust, they will learn to trust the world that waits beyond our walls. Then, when the time comes, I know I will be able to trust them, too, and let them go. Loving them, I grow. Growing, they learn to give love back.

A Note to Readers

★★The Chinaberry catalog is a wonderful resource for children's books, adult books, simple crafts, and other items that "support families in raising their children with love, honesty, and joy to be reverent, loving caretakers of each other and the earth." To order a catalog, call 1-800-776-2242.

★★TableTalk and KidTalk cards are available at better toy stores or by calling 1-800-997-5676.

★★*Mothering* magazine "celebrates the experience of mothering and fathering as something worthy of one's best efforts and seeks to inspire a recognition of the immense importance and value of parenting and family life in the development of the full potential of parents as well as children." When my children were younger, the arrival of *Mothering* in my mailbox would be the highlight of a day. Although I did not always agree with the opinions expressed, I was always challenged and motivated by the message. To order a subscription, call 1-800-984-8116.

**Readers interested in learning more about Waldorf education may contact the Association of Waldorf Schools in North America, 3911 Bannister Road, Fair Oaks, CA 95628 (phone: 916-961-0927). A good introductory book is *Waldorf Education: A Family Guide,* edited by Pamela Johnson and Karen L. Rivers, published by Michaelmas Press, PO Box 702, Amesbury, MA 01913-0016.

**Nancy Mellon's fine books are available through your local bookstore or from the publishers: *The Art of Storytelling,* Element, Boston, MA (1998), and *Storytelling for Parents,* Hawthorn Press, Stroud, Gloucestershire, U.K. (2000).

Acknowledgment*s*

Many of the ideas in this book have their roots in the work of Rudolph Steiner, an Austrian educator who founded the first Waldorf School in 1919. The Waldorf philosophy of child development and the reverence for all life that underlies Waldorf education have guided and shaped my family's life from the time my children were small. As our world grows increasingly complex, and as our children confront more stresses at ever earlier ages, the vision of Rudolph Steiner seems all the more relevant. Certainly his wisdom has provided my husband and me with a solid foundation upon which to build our own approach to parenting.

I am grateful to all the mothers whose lives and words have inspired me, but especially to Carol Cashion and Michele Wickerham, the moms in my own backyard. Day in, day out, we do this work together, and they have often mothered my own two boys while I was upstairs writing about them. To those good friends who have read bits and pieces of this book at various stages, thank you, for your responses helped me find my way: Carol and Michele, again, as well as Norma Duncan, Richard Eder, Lisa Freeman, Nancy Heselton, Gish Jen, Nancy Mellon, Elivia Sagov, Becky Saikia-Wilson, Linda Weltner, and Debra Woods. Special thanks, too, to my mother, Marilyn Kenison; my agents, Mary Evans and Tanya McKinnon; Jennifer Romanello at Time Warner; and to my dear friend, fellow mother, and beloved editor, Jamie Raab.

Finally, heartfelt thanks to my husband, Steven Lewers, who lived this book and believed that I could write it.

ABOUT THE AUTHOR

Katrina Kenison grew up in Milford, New Hampshire, and graduated from Smith College in 1980. A former editor at Houghton Mifflin Company, she has been the annual editor of *The Best American Short Stories* anthology since 1990. She is coeditor, with John Updike, of *The Best American Short Stories of the Century,* published by Houghton Mifflin in 1999. She is also coeditor of *Mothers: Twenty Stories of Contemporary Motherhood,* published in 1996 by Farrar, Straus & Giroux. *Mitten Strings for God* is her first book.

Katrina Kenison lives outside of Boston with her husband, Steven Lewers, and their two sons.